ADORATION PRAYERS

Written and compiled
by Marie Paul Curley, FSP

Edited by Mary Leonora Wilson, FSP

BOOKS & MEDIA

Boston

Nihil Obstat: Reverend Joseph Briody, S.S.L., S.T.D.

Imprimatur: ✠ Seán P. Cardinal O'Malley, O.F.M. Cap.
　　　　　　Archbishop of Boston
　　　　　　May 10, 2023

Library of Congress Cataloging-in-Publication Data Number: 2023942241

ISBN 10: 0-8198-2416-X
ISBN 13: 978-0-8198-2416-5

Cover art and design by Kenneth Reaume

Published by Pauline Books & Media, 50 Saint Paul's Avenue, Boston, MA 02130–3491

Printed in the U.S.A.

www.pauline.org

Pauline Books & Media is the publishing house of the Daughters of St. Paul, an international congregation of women religious serving the Church with the communications media.

1 2 3 4 5 6 7 8 9　　　　　　32 31 30 29 28 27 26 25 24

Contents

INTRODUCTION

Jesus Living Among Us

In addition to suffering and dying on the Cross for our salvation, Jesus left us yet another amazing gift: the gift of himself—Body, Blood, soul, and divinity—in the sacrament of the Holy Eucharist. In this incredible way our Lord secured his living presence among us, just as he promised: "Remember, I am with you always, to the end of the age" (Mt 28:20). With this gift of himself he feeds, strengthens, sanctifies, encourages, comforts, and accompanies us. We are never alone.

Because he desired to remain with us in this way, Jesus commanded his apostles to perpetuate this sacrament for all times: "This is my body, which is given for you. Do this in remembrance of me" (Lk 22:19). The apostles were faithful to this divine commission. Following that Last Supper, they and those they consecrated to the ministerial priesthood and all their successors since then, have continued to offer the Holy Sacrifice of the Mass, providing us, in the name of Jesus and through the action of the Holy Spirit, with the Body and Blood of Christ.

In the Eucharist, Jesus communicates his very own life to us. We have his word:

Those who eat my flesh and drink my blood have eternal life, and I will raise them up on the last day; for my flesh is true food and my blood is true drink. Those who eat my flesh and drink my blood abide in me, and I in them. Just as the living Father sent me, and I live because of the Father, so whoever eats me will live because of me. (Jn 6:54–57)

We call this presence sacramental—Jesus Christ, resurrected and living in the Blessed Sacrament.

What is more, Jesus continues to be present sacramentally not only during the Mass, but wherever the consecrated hosts are kept—in the tabernacles of Catholic churches throughout the world. How can we lament the thought that the Lord no longer walks the streets of Palestine, when he lives in fact in our very own neighborhood and waits for us to come and visit? He wants us to come with all our needs, our anxieties, our doubts, our difficulties, yes, even with our sinfulness, so that he can heal, restore and strengthen us. He wants to make his love known to us and hear about our desire to love him. He wants to be our intimate Friend, our Teacher, and he only asks that we spend time with him.

Jesus is not only the Head of the Church but, in the Blessed Sacrament especially, he is the Heart of the Church. All the saints were devoted to Christ in the most Holy Eucharist. This little book gathers together Eucharistic prayers from saints and faithful Christians of all ages right to the present day. May it be an inspiration, a springboard, so to speak, for our own prayer of adoration and love for Jesus in the Eucharist. And may the love that fills the Eucharistic Heart of Jesus transform our hearts as we grow in intimate friendship with the Lord and share that loving friendship with the people around us.

MARY LEONORA WILSON, FSP

Praying with the Bible

Holy Scripture will be our most prized reading;
this letter from our heavenly Father
invites us to heaven,
communicating to us his secrets,
his most lovable truths,
his designs for us.

—Blessed James Alberione

The Beauty and Power of God's Word

In the library of books contained in the Bible, God reveals himself, the purpose of our existence, and the way to true happiness. Isn't this reason enough to find a Bible and open it? Yet, many of us don't open the Bible because we are too unfamiliar with it or intimidated by it.

Psalm 119 eloquently portrays the word of God as:

life-giving,
comforting,
precious,
a promise,
a song,
a delight,
giving understanding,
a lamp or light,
joy of our hearts,
our hope,
our safety.

We all want the life, comfort, treasure, promise, strength, and joy that reading and praying with the word of God can give. Because the Bible *is* the very word of God, it is active whenever we encounter it. God *always* speaks to us through his word.

God's word is one of the privileged, sure ways that we can get to know God's heart. By hearing God's desires and designs for us, we can truly come to know God.

Prayerfully Listening to God's Word

For many people, the Bible is an untapped treasure that needs to be unlocked with a secret key. There *is* a secret key to praying with the Bible, and it is this: knowing that God *wants* to communicate with us.

Because the Bible is God's word to us, we only need to open our hearts and truly listen. Not a passive "just being there," but a listening that is thirsty, that hangs on every syllable; a listening as eager as that of those in love who wait to catch the first whispered affirmations of their beloved's love.

Don't be afraid to slow down, read, and listen in a way that is truly receptive to God's invitational message of love: "You are precious to me," "I love you," "Remain in me," "Rest in me," "Follow me," "Seek first the kingdom of God," etc.

However you decide to read, study, and pray with the word of God, what is most important is to be open and let it shape your life, attitudes, and prayer. The biblical prayers included here are just a small selection of some of the most familiar. Your Bible is the best possible resource you can bring to your prayer before Jesus in the Holy Eucharist.

Blessed James Alberione believed that praying with the Bible before the Blessed Sacrament brought special graces and that the word of God and the Eucharist should be inseparable in our hearts.

The Bible . . .
is the great sacrament of God's word.
Within its pages
the divine fire of the Holy Spirit burns,
just as under the sacramental species
the divine Person of Christ lives.
And just as the person
who receives the Host
is nourished by divine food that gives
a strength unequalled by any other,
so too the person who is nourished
by the words of the Bible
experiences interiorly
the kindling of a divine fire
which causes an activity
that cannot be expressed,
one which pervades his or her being
and spiritually renews it.

The person who eats the Bread of Life
will live eternally.
When we nourish ourselves
on the word of the Bible
with the right dispositions,
we will be permeated by the Holy Spirit.[1]

Biblical Prayers

Psalm 23

The LORD is my shepherd; I shall not want.
     He makes me lie down in green pastures.
He leads me beside still waters.
     He restores my soul.
He leads me in paths of righteousness
     for his name's sake.

Even though I walk through the valley of the
    shadow of death,
     I will fear no evil,
for you are with me;
     your rod and your staff,
     they comfort me.

You prepare a table before me
     in the presence of my enemies;
you anoint my head with oil;
     my cup overflows.

Surely goodness and mercy shall follow me
  all the days of my life,
and I shall dwell in the house of the Lord forever.

Psalm 51

Have mercy on me, O God,
  according to your steadfast love;
according to your abundant mercy
  blot out my transgressions.
Wash me thoroughly from my iniquity,
  and cleanse me from my sin!

For I know my transgressions,
  and my sin is ever before me.
Against you, you only, have I sinned
  and done what is evil in your sight,
so that you may be justified in your words
  and blameless in your judgment.
Behold, I was brought forth in iniquity,
  and in sin did my mother conceive me.
Behold, you delight in truth in the inward being,
  and you teach me wisdom in the secret
    heart.

Purge me with hyssop, and I shall be clean;
  wash me, and I shall be whiter than snow.

Let me hear joy and gladness;
    let the bones that you have broken rejoice.
Hide your face from my sins,
    and blot out all my iniquities.
Create in me a clean heart, O God,
    and renew a right spirit within me.
Cast me not away from your presence,
    and take not your Holy Spirit from me.
Restore to me the joy of your salvation,
    and uphold me with a willing spirit.

Then I will teach transgressors your ways,
    and sinners will return to you.
Deliver me from bloodguiltiness, O God,
        O God of my salvation,
        and my tongue will sing aloud of your
            righteousness.
O Lord, open my lips,
    and my mouth will declare your praise.
For you will not delight in sacrifice, or I would
    give it;
        you will not be pleased with a burnt
            offering.
The sacrifices of God are a broken spirit;
    a broken and contrite heart, O God, you
        will not despise.

Do good to Zion in your good pleasure;
>   build up the walls of Jerusalem;
then will you delight in right sacrifices,
>   in burnt offerings and whole burnt
>   offerings;
>   then bulls will be offered on your altar.

Psalm 63

O God, you are my God; earnestly I seek you;
>   my soul thirsts for you;
my flesh faints for you,
>   as in a dry and weary land where there is
>   no water.
So I have looked upon you in the sanctuary,
>   beholding your power and glory.
Because your steadfast love is better than life,
>   my lips will praise you.
So I will bless you as long as I live;
>   in your name I will lift up my hands.

My soul will be satisfied as with fat and
> rich food,
>   and my mouth will praise you with joyful
>   lips,
when I remember you upon my bed,

and meditate on you in the watches of
the night;
for you have been my help,
and in the shadow of your wings I will
sing for joy.
My soul clings to you;
your right hand upholds me.

Psalm 100

Make a joyful noise to the LORD, all the earth!
Serve the LORD with gladness!
Come into his presence with singing!

Know that the LORD, he is God!
It is he who made us, and we are his;
we are his people, and the sheep of his
pasture.

Enter his gates with thanksgiving,
and his courts with praise!
Give thanks to him; bless his name!

For the LORD is good;
his steadfast love endures forever,
and his faithfulness to all generations.

Psalm 116

I love the LORD, because he has heard
      my voice and my pleas for mercy.
Because he inclined his ear to me,
      therefore I will call on him as long
         as I live.
The snares of death encompassed me;
      the pangs of Sheol laid hold on me;
      I suffered distress and anguish.
Then I called on the name of the LORD:
      "O LORD, I pray, deliver my soul!"

Gracious is the LORD, and righteous;
      our God is merciful.
The LORD preserves the simple;
      when I was brought low, he saved me.
Return, O my soul, to your rest;
      for the LORD has dealt bountifully with you.

For you have delivered my soul from death,
      my eyes from tears,
      my feet from stumbling;
I will walk before the LORD
      in the land of the living.

I believed, even when I spoke:
     "I am greatly afflicted";
I said in my alarm,
     "All mankind are liars."

What shall I render to the LORD
     for all his benefits to me?
I will lift up the cup of salvation
     and call on the name of the LORD,
I will pay my vows to the LORD
     in the presence of all his people.

Precious in the sight of the LORD
     is the death of his saints.
O LORD, I am your servant;
     I am your servant, the son of your maid-
         servant.
     You have loosed my bonds.
I will offer to you the sacrifice of thanksgiving
     and call on the name of the LORD.
I will pay my vows to the LORD
     in the presence of all his people,
in the courts of the house of the LORD,
     in your midst, O Jerusalem.
Praise the LORD!

Psalm 130

Out of the depths I cry to you, O LORD!
    O Lord, hear my voice!
Let your ears be attentive
    to the voice of my pleas for mercy!

If you, O LORD, should mark iniquities,
    O Lord, who could stand?
But with you there is forgiveness,
    that you may be feared.

I wait for the LORD, my soul waits,
    and in his word I hope;
my soul waits for the Lord
    more than watchmen for the morning,
    more than watchmen for the morning.

O Israel, hope in the LORD!
    For with the LORD there is steadfast love,
    and with him is plentiful redemption.
And he will redeem Israel
    from all his iniquities.

Psalm 139

O LORD, you have searched me and known me!
You know when I sit down and when I rise up;

you discern my thoughts from afar.
You search out my path and my lying down
and are acquainted with all my ways.
Even before a word is on my tongue,
behold, O LORD, you know it altogether.
You hem me in, behind and before,
and lay your hand upon me.
Such knowledge is too wonderful for me;
it is high; I cannot attain it.

Where shall I go from your Spirit?
Or where shall I flee from your presence?
If I ascend to heaven, you are there!
If I make my bed in Sheol, you are there!
If I take the wings of the morning
and dwell in the uttermost parts of the sea,
even there your hand shall lead me,
and your right hand shall hold me.
If I say, "Surely the darkness shall cover me,
and the light about me be night,"
even the darkness is not dark to you;
the night is bright as the day,
for darkness is as light with you.

For you formed my inward parts;
you knitted me together in my mother's
womb.

I praise you, for I am fearfully and wonderfully
    made.
Wonderful are your works;
       my soul knows it very well.
My frame was not hidden from you,
when I was being made in secret,
         intricately woven in the depths of the
           earth.
Your eyes saw my unformed substance;
in your book were written, every one of them,
        the days that were formed for me,
         when as yet there was none of them.

How precious to me are your thoughts, O God!
       How vast is the sum of them!
If I would count them, they are more than the
    sand.
       I awake, and I am still with you.

Oh that you would slay the wicked, O God!
       O men of blood, depart from me!
They speak against you with malicious intent;
       your enemies take your name in vain.
Do I not hate those who hate you, O LORD?
       And do I not loathe those who rise up
         against you?

I hate them with complete hatred;
     I count them my enemies.

Search me, O God, and know my heart!
     Try me and know my thoughts!
And see if there be any grievous way in me,
     and lead me in the way everlasting!

Canticle of Isaiah 55

"Come, everyone who thirsts,
     come to the waters;
and he who has no money,
     come, buy and eat!
Come, buy wine and milk
     without money and without price.
Why do you spend your money for that which is
   not bread,
     and your labor for that which does not
       satisfy?
Listen diligently to me, and eat what is good,
     and delight yourselves in rich food.
Incline your ear, and come to me;
     hear, that your soul may live;
and I will make with you an everlasting covenant,
     my steadfast, sure love for David.

Behold, I made him a witness to the peoples,
>   a leader and commander for the peoples.
Behold, you shall call a nation that you do not
    know,
>   and a nation that did not know you shall
>   run to you,
because of the LORD your God, and of the Holy
    One of Israel,
>   for he has glorified you.

"Seek the LORD while he may be found;
>   call upon him while he is near;
let the wicked forsake his way,
>   and the unrighteous man his thoughts;
let him return to the LORD, that he may have
    compassion on him,
>   and to our God, for he will abundantly
>   pardon.
For my thoughts are not your thoughts,
>   neither are your ways my ways, declares
>   the LORD.
For as the heavens are higher than the earth,
>   so are my ways higher than your ways
>   and my thoughts than your thoughts.

"For as the rain and the snow come down from
    heaven

and do not return there but water the
earth,
making it bring forth and sprout,
giving seed to the sower and bread to the
eater,
so shall my word be that goes out from my mouth;
it shall not return to me empty,
but it shall accomplish that which I purpose,
and shall succeed in the thing for which
I sent it.

"For you shall go out in joy
and be led forth in peace;
the mountains and the hills before you
shall break forth into singing,
and all the trees of the field shall clap
their hands.
Instead of the thorn shall come up the cypress;
instead of the brier shall come up the
myrtle;
and it shall make a name for the LORD,
an everlasting sign that shall not be cut off."

Benedictus

Blessed be the Lord God of Israel,
> for he has visited and redeemed his people
and has raised up a horn of salvation for us
> in the house of his servant David,
as he spoke by the mouth of his holy
> prophets from of old,
that we should be saved from our enemies
> and from the hand of all who hate us;
to show the mercy promised to our fathers
> and to remember his holy covenant,
the oath that he swore to our father Abraham, to
> grant us
>> that we, being delivered from the hand of
>> our enemies,
might serve him without fear,
> in holiness and righteousness before him
> all our days.
And you, child, will be called the prophet of the
> Most High;
>> for you will go before the Lord to prepare
>> his ways,
to give knowledge of salvation to his people
> in the forgiveness of their sins,

because of the tender mercy of our God,
> whereby the sunrise shall visit us from on
> > high
to give light to those who sit in darkness and in
> the shadow of death,
> > to guide our feet into the way of peace.

Luke 1:68–79

Magnificat

My soul magnifies the Lord,
> and my spirit rejoices in God my Savior,
for he has looked on the humble estate of his
> servant.
> > For behold, from now on all generations
> > > will call me blessed;
for he who is mighty has done great things for me,
> and holy is his name.
And his mercy is for those who fear him
> from generation to generation.
He has shown strength with his arm;
> > he has scattered the proud in the thoughts
> > > of their hearts;
he has brought down the mighty from their
> thrones

and exalted those of humble estate;
he has filled the hungry with good things,
    and the rich he has sent away empty.
He has helped his servant Israel,
    in remembrance of his mercy,
as he spoke to our fathers,
    to Abraham and to his offspring forever.

Luke 1:46–55

Jesus' Priestly Prayer

"Father, the hour has come; glorify your Son so that the Son may glorify you, since you have given him authority over all people, to give eternal life to all whom you have given him. And this is eternal life, that they may know you, the only true God, and Jesus Christ whom you have sent. I glorified you on earth by finishing the work that you gave me to do. So now, Father, glorify me in your own presence with the glory that I had in your presence before the world existed.

"I have made your name known to those whom you gave me from the world. They were yours, and you gave them to me, and they have kept your word. Now they know that everything you have given me is from you; for the words that you gave to me I have given to them, and they have received them and know in truth that I came from you; and they have believed that you sent me. I am asking on their behalf; I am not asking on behalf of the world, but on behalf of those whom you gave me, because they are yours. All mine are yours, and yours are mine; and I have been glorified in them. And now I am no longer in the world, but they are in the world, and I am coming to you. Holy Father, protect them in your name that you have given me, so that they may be one, as we are one. While I was with them, I protected them in your name that you have given me. I guarded them, and not one of them was lost except the one destined to be lost, so that the scripture might be fulfilled. But now I am coming to you, and I speak these things in the world so that they may have my joy made complete in themselves. I have given them your word, and the world has hated them because they do not belong to the world, just as I do not belong to the world. I am not asking you to take them out of the world, but I ask you to protect them from the evil one. They do not belong to the world, just as I do not belong to the world. Sanctify them in the truth; your word is truth. As you have sent me into the world, so I have sent them into the world. And for their sakes I sanctify myself, so that they also may be sanctified in truth.

"I ask not only on behalf of these, but also on behalf of those who will believe in me through their word, that they may all be one. As you, Father, are in me and I am in you, may they also be in us, so that the world may believe that you have sent me. The glory that you have given me I have given them, so that they may be one, as we are one, I in them and you in me, that they may become completely one, so that the world may know that you have sent me and have loved them even as you have loved me. Father, I desire that those also, whom you have given me, may be with me where I am, to see my glory, which you have given me because you loved me before the foundation of the world.

"Righteous Father, the world does not know you, but I know you; and these know that you have sent me. I made your name known to them, and I will make it known, so that the love with which you have loved me may be in them, and I in them."

John 17:1–26

Canticle of Ephesians 1

Blessed be the God and Father of our Lord Jesus Christ, who has blessed us in Christ with every spiritual blessing in the heavenly places, even as he chose us in him before the foundation of the world, that we should be holy and blameless before him. In love he predestined us for adoption to himself as sons through Jesus Christ, according to the purpose of his will, to the praise of his glorious grace, with which he has blessed us in the Beloved. In him we have redemption through his blood, the forgiveness of our trespasses, according to the riches of his grace, which he lavished upon us, in all wisdom and insight making known to us the mystery of his will, according to his purpose, which he set forth in Christ as a plan for the fullness of time, to unite all things in him, things in heaven and things on earth.

In him we have obtained an inheritance, having been predestined according to the purpose of him who works all things according to the counsel of his will, so that we who were the first to hope in Christ might be to the praise of his glory. In him you also, when you heard the word of truth, the gospel of your salvation, and believed in him, were sealed with the promised Holy Spirit, who is the guarantee of our inheritance until we acquire possession of it, to the praise of his glory.

Ephesians 1:3–14

Canticle of 1 Peter

Blessed be the God and Father of our Lord Jesus Christ! According to his great mercy, he has caused us to be born again to a living hope through the resurrection of Jesus Christ from the dead, to an inheritance that is imperishable, undefiled, and unfading, kept in heaven for you, who by God's power are being guarded through faith for a salvation ready to be revealed in the last time. In this you rejoice, though now for a little while, if necessary, you have been grieved by various trials, so that the tested genuineness of your faith—more precious than gold that perishes though it is tested by fire—may be found to result in praise and glory and honor at the revelation of Jesus Christ. Though you have not seen him, you love him. Though you do not now see him, you believe in him and rejoice with joy that is inexpressible and filled with glory, obtaining the outcome of your faith, the salvation of your souls.

1 Peter 1:3–9

Canticle of Revelation 19

*This Canticle is made up of excerpts from the heavenly songs
John hears.*

Hallelujah!
Salvation and glory and power belong to our God,
for his judgments are true and just . . .

Hallelujah!
. . . Praise our God,
all you his servants,
you who fear him,
small and great. . . .

Hallelujah!
For the Lord our God
the Almighty reigns.
Let us rejoice and exult
and give him the glory,
for the marriage of the Lamb has come,
and his Bride has made herself ready.

Revelation 19:1–3, 5–7

Prayers of Adoration

Adoration is the foundation of our relationship with our Creator, the all-good, all-knowing, all-beautiful Lord. Adoration is wondering love: a spontaneous response to the God who loves us beyond our understanding.

What kind of response dare we give to the Almighty, who humbly and mysteriously gives himself to us in the Holy Eucharist?

Our awe, wonder, reverence, love, and delight —none are truly worthy of the Lord of heaven and earth, yet they are precious to God because they come from our hearts.

> May I never leave you there alone but be wholly present, my faith wholly vigilant, wholly adoring, and wholly surrendered to your creative action.
>
> —Saint Elizabeth of the Trinity

Morning Offering

The Morning Offering is a deeply Eucharistic prayer, setting the tone for the whole day.

Divine Heart of Jesus, through the Immaculate Heart of Mary, I offer you my prayers, works, joys, and sufferings of this day, for all the intentions of your Sacred Heart, in union with the Holy Sacrifice of the Mass throughout the world, for the salvation of souls, the reparation of sins, the reunion of all Christians, and for the intentions of the Holy Father recommended this month.

Prayer of Adoration

Jesus, today's adoration is the meeting of my soul
and my entire being with you.
I am the creature meeting you, my Creator;
the disciple before the Divine Master;
the patient with the Doctor of souls;
the poor one appealing to the Rich One;
the thirsty one drinking at the Font;
the weak one before the Almighty;
the tempted seeking a sure Refuge;
the blind person searching for the Light;
the friend who goes to the True Friend;

the lost sheep sought by the Divine Shepherd;
the wayward heart who finds the Way;
the unenlightened one who finds Wisdom;
the bride who finds the Spouse of the soul;
the "nothing" who finds the All;
the afflicted who finds the Consoler;
the seeker who finds life's meaning.

Adapted from Blessed James Alberione

Prayer of Presence

Lord, I come before you here in the Eucharist, and believe that you are looking at me and listening to my prayer. You are so great and so holy, I adore you. You have given me everything, I thank you. I have sinned against you, and I ask your pardon with a heart full of sorrow. You are rich in mercy; I ask you to grant me all the graces that will help me draw closer to you.

You

You are the peace of all things calm.
You are the place to hide from harm.
You are the light that shines in the dark.
You are the heart's eternal spark.

You are the door that's open wide.
You are the guest who waits inside.
You are the stranger at the door.
You are the calling of the poor.
You are the light, the truth, the way.
You are my Savior this very day.

An ancient Celtic blessing

Chaplet to Jesus Master, Way, Truth, and Life

1. Jesus, Divine Master, we adore you as the Word Incarnate sent by the Father to instruct us in life-giving truths. You are uncreated Truth, the only Master. You alone have words of eternal life. We thank you for having imparted to us the light of reason and the light of faith, and for having called us to the light of glory. We believe, submitting our whole mind to you and to the Church. Master, show us the treasures of your wisdom, let us know the Father, make us your true disciples. Increase our faith so that we may attain to the eternal vision in heaven.

Jesus Master, Way, Truth, and Life, have mercy on us.

2. Jesus, Divine Master, we adore you as the Beloved of the Father, the sole Way to him. We thank you because you made yourself our model. You left us examples of the highest perfection. You have invited us to follow you on earth and in heaven. We contemplate you in the various periods of your earthly life. We docilely place ourselves in your school and follow your teachings. Draw us to you so that by following in your footsteps and renouncing ourselves, we may seek only your will. Increase active hope in us, the desire to be found similar to you at the judgment, and to possess you forever in heaven.

Jesus Master, Way, Truth, and Life, have mercy on us.

3. Jesus, Divine Master, we adore you as the only-begotten Son of God, come on the earth to give life, the most abundant life, to humanity. We thank you because by dying on the Cross, you merited life for us, which you give us in Baptism and nourish in the Eucharist and in the other sacraments. Live in us, O Jesus, with the outpouring of the Holy Spirit, so that we may love you with our whole mind, strength, and heart, and love our neighbor as ourselves for love of you. Increase charity in us, so that one day, called from the sepulcher to the glorious life, we

may be united with you in the eternal happiness of heaven.

Jesus Master, Way, Truth, and Life, have mercy on us.

4. Jesus, Divine Master, we adore you living in the Church, your Mystical Body and our sole ark of salvation. We thank you for having given us this infallible and indefectible Mother, in whom you continue to be for humanity the Way, the Truth, and the Life. We ask of you that those who do not believe may come to her inextinguishable light, the erring return to her, and all people be united in faith, in a common hope, in charity. Exalt the Church, assist the Pope, sanctify the clergy and those consecrated to you. Lord Jesus, our wish is yours: that there be one fold under one Shepherd, so that we may all be reunited in the Church exultant in heaven.

Jesus Master, Way, Truth, and Life, have mercy on us.

5. Jesus, Divine Master, we adore you with the angels who sang the reasons for your Incarnation: "Glory to God and peace to all people." We thank you for having called us to share in your own apostolate. Enkindle in us your own flame of zeal for

God and for souls. Fill all our powers with yourself. Live in us so that we may radiate you through our apostolate of prayer and suffering, of the media and of the word, of example and of deed. Send good laborers into your harvest. Enlighten preachers, teachers, and writers; infuse in them the Holy Spirit with his seven gifts; dispose minds and hearts to receive him. Come, Master and Lord! Teach and reign through Mary, Mother, Teacher, and Queen.

Jesus Master, Way, Truth, and Life, have mercy on us.

Blessed James Alberione

Chaplet of Eucharistic Adoration

Make the Sign of the Cross and pray the Eucharistic prayer of the angel at Fatima:

Most Holy Trinity, I adore you! My God, I love you in the most Blessed Sacrament.

The chaplet can be prayed with or without beads. The chaplet beads are made up of one single bead, three beads, and then a circle of three sets of ten beads each time preceded by a single bead. On the first single bead, pray:

I adore you, Eucharistic Jesus, present in so many tabernacles throughout the world. I unite myself to you in love, especially in those churches where you are abandoned and neglected.

On the three beads that follow, pray:

Jesus in the Holy Eucharist, you are eternal Truth; I believe in you.

Jesus in the Holy Eucharist, you are the Way of salvation; I hope in you.

Jesus in the Holy Eucharist, you are my Life; I love you with all my heart above all things and unite myself to you in the Blessed Sacrament.

On the centerpiece medal make an act of spiritual communion.

On the single beads between the decades, pray:

Father, Son, and Holy Spirit, I praise and thank you for your great love manifest in your precious gift of the most Holy Eucharist; may it be known, honored, and adored by everyone.

On the sets of 10 beads, pray:

Eucharistic Jesus, my Way, Truth, and Life, truly present in the most Blessed Sacrament of the altar, I adore you, love you, and unite myself to you in all the tabernacles throughout the world.

Conclude the chaplet with the Divine Praises (see page 153).

Mary Leonora Wilson, FSP

Bread of My Soul

I place myself in the presence of him, in whose Incarnate Presence I am before I place myself there.

I adore you, my Savior, present here as God and man, in soul and Body, in true flesh and Blood.

I acknowledge and confess that I kneel before that sacred humanity, who was conceived in Mary's womb and lay in Mary's bosom; who grew up to man's estate, and by the Sea of Galilee called the Twelve, wrought miracles, and spoke words of wisdom and peace; who in due season hung on the cross, lay in the tomb, rose from the dead, and now reigns in heaven.

I praise, and bless, and give myself wholly to him, who is the true Bread of my soul, and my everlasting joy.

Saint John Henry Newman

We Adore You

We adore you, most holy Lord Jesus Christ, here and in all your churches throughout the world. We bless you, because by your holy Cross you have redeemed the world.

Attributed to Saint Francis of Assisi

Immersed in Adoration

I adore you, Lord and Creator, hidden in the Blessed Sacrament. I adore you for all the works of your hands that reveal to me so much wisdom, goodness, and mercy, O Lord. You have spread so much beauty over the earth, and it tells me about your beauty, even though these beautiful things are but a faint reflection of you, incomprehensible Beauty. And although you have hidden yourself and concealed your beauty, my eye, enlightened by faith, reaches you and I recognize my Creator, my highest Good, and my heart is completely immersed in prayer of adoration.

Saint Faustina Kowalska[2]

Beloved Jesus

Beloved Jesus, I believe that you are truly present here in the Eucharist.

I adore you.

You look at me and listen to me as I look at you and listen to you.

I love you.

You have given me everything that I am and have. Thank you.

Please open my heart and mind so that our visit together may be a time of union and love and that I may be transformed in you, my Teacher and Master. Amen.

Patricia Cora Shaules, FSP

Stay with Me, Lord

Stay with me, Lord, for it is necessary to have you present so that I do not forget you.

Stay with me, Lord, because I am weak and I need your strength, that I may not fall so often.

Stay with me, Lord, for you are my life, and without you, I am without fervor.

Stay with me, Lord, for you are my light, and without you, I am in darkness.

Stay with me, Lord, to show me your will.

Stay with me, Lord, so that I hear your voice and follow you.

Stay with me, Lord, for I desire to love you very much, and always be in your company.

Stay with me, Lord, if you wish me to be faithful to you.

Stay with me, Lord, for as poor as my soul is, I wish it to be a place of consolation for you, a nest of love . . .

Stay with me tonight, Jesus, in life with all its dangers, I need you.

Let me recognize you as your disciples did at the breaking of bread, so that Eucharistic Communion may be the light that disperses the darkness, the force that sustains me, the unique joy of my heart . . .

Stay with me, Lord, for it is you alone I look for. Your love, your grace, your will, your heart, your Spirit, because I love you and ask no other reward but to love you more and more.

With a firm love, I will love you with all my heart. Amen.

Saint Pio of Pietrelcina[3]

Act of Abandonment

You, O my God, always think of me.
You are within me, outside of me.
I am written on the palm of your hand.
O Lord, that I may always and in all things
do your will.
O Lord, I abandon myself in you.
No worries.
I abandon myself completely in you, always.

Venerable Thecla Merlo, FSP

Act of Adoration

Jesus, my God, I adore you
here present in the Blessed Sacrament of the altar,
where you wait day and night to be our comfort
while we await
your unveiled presence in heaven.

Jesus, my God, I adore you
in all places where the Blessed Sacrament
is reserved,
and where sins are committed against this
Sacrament of Love.

Jesus, my God, I adore you for all time,
past, present, and future,
for every soul that ever was, is, or shall be created.

Jesus, my God,
who for us endured hunger and cold, labor,
    and fatigue,
I adore you.

Jesus, my God,
who for my sake deigned to subject yourself to
    the humiliation of temptation,
to the betrayal and defection of friends,
to the scorn of your enemies,
I adore you.

Jesus, my God,
who for us endured the buffeting of your passion,
the scourging,
the crowning with thorns,
the heavy weight of the Cross,
I adore you.

Jesus, my God, who, for my salvation and that of
    the whole human race,
was cruelly nailed to the Cross

and hung there for three long hours in bitter
    agony,
I adore you.

Jesus, my God, who for love of us instituted this
    Blessed Sacrament
and offered your life for the sins of the whole
    world,
I adore you.

Jesus, my God,
who in Holy Communion became the food of
    my soul,
I adore you.

Jesus, for you I live.
Jesus, for you I die.
Jesus, I am all yours in life and death. Amen.

Cardinal John J. Carberry[4]

Litany of the Most Blessed Sacrament

This litany's descriptions of the Eucharist can move hearts to deeper adoration. Feel free to adapt the response from "have mercy on us," to something that appeals to you personally, such as "we adore you," "we love you," or "we trust in you."

Lord, have mercy on us.
　R̸. *Christ, have mercy on us.*
Lord, have mercy on us. Christ, hear us.
　R̸. *Christ, graciously hear us.*
God, the Father of heaven,
　R̸. *have mercy on us.*
God the Son, Redeemer of the world, R̸.
God the Holy Spirit, R̸.
Holy Trinity, one God, R̸.
Jesus, living Bread come down from heaven, R̸.
Jesus, Bread from heaven giving life to the world, R̸.
Jesus, hidden God and Savior, R̸.
Jesus, who has loved us with an everlasting love, R̸.
Jesus, whose delight is to be with the children of men, R̸.

Jesus, who gave your flesh for the life of the world, R̰.

Jesus, who invites all to come to you, R̰.

Jesus, who promises eternal life to those
who receive your Body and Blood, R̰.

Jesus, ever ready to welcome us to the table
of the Eucharist, R̰.

Jesus, who stands knocking at the door of
our hearts, R̰.

Jesus, who welcomes us and blesses us, R̰.

Jesus, who allows us to sit at your feet with
Mary of Bethany, R̰.

Jesus, who invites us to follow you as your
disciples, R̰.

Jesus, who has not left us orphans, R̰.

Sacrament of love, R̰.

Sacrament of all goodness, R̰.

Sacrament of strength, R̰.

Sacrament of nourishing grace, R̰.

That you reveal yourself to us in the breaking
of bread as you did to the two disciples at
Emmaus, R̰. *we beseech you, hear us.*

That you bless us who have not seen and yet have
believed, R̰.

That we may love you with all our heart, all our
    soul, all our mind, and all our strength, R.

That the fruit of each Communion may be to love
    others for love of you, R.

That our one desire may be to love you and
    to do your will, R.

That we may forever remain in your love, R.

That you would teach us to pray as you taught your
    disciples, R.

That you grant us every virtue for right living, R.

That throughout this day you will keep us closely
    united to you, R.

That you give us the grace to persevere to
    the end, R.

That you be our comfort and support in our final
    hours, R.

That you deliver us safely into the arms of our heav-
    enly Father, R.

Lamb of God, you take away the sins of the world,
    spare us, O Lord.

Lamb of God, you take away the sins of the world,
    graciously hear us, O Lord.

Lamb of God, you take away the sins of the world,
have mercy on us.

Let us pray.

Heavenly Father, you draw us to yourself through the wondrous Eucharistic mystery. Grant us a strong and lively faith in this Sacrament of love in which your Son Jesus Christ is present, offered, and received. We ask this through the same Christ our Lord. Amen.

Credo, Adoro, Amo

I Believe, I Adore, I Love

Credo: I believe, Lord, that you are truly, substantially present in the Blessed Sacrament: the same God incarnate who became like us in all things, except sin, and redeemed us by your supreme act of love on Calvary.

Credo: I believe. What else could I do? You have the words of eternal life: "Take this, all of you, and eat it; this is my Body. Take this, all of you, and drink from it; this is the cup of my Blood, the Blood of the new and everlasting covenant. It will be shed for you and for all so that sins may be forgiven."

Credo: I believe, Lord, increase my faith.

Adoro: I adore you, Lord, the Alpha and the Omega, the Beginning and the End of my life, without whose Divine Providence I could not draw a breath or move a limb.

All that I am, all that I have, I owe to you. Without you I am nothing and can do nothing. You are my God and my all. Help me to be totally dedicated to you.

I offer myself as your hands and feet to run errands of charity in your name. Yes, I give myself to you as a living tool in your hands—as your servant, if need be.

Adoro: I adore you, O Lord, with every fiber of my being.

Amo: I love you, O Lord, with my whole heart and soul, not for what you will give me but for what you are—Infinite Love. If I cannot love you with the immaculate love of your Blessed Mother, give me the grace to love you with the penitent heart of a Magdalen. If I cannot love you with the angelic love of a Saint John, give me the grace to love you with the penitent heart of a Peter.

Amo: I love you, O Lord, with my whole heart and soul.

Richard Cardinal Cushing

Loving Lord, I Believe

Loving Lord, I believe that you are truly present—Body, Blood, soul, and divinity—in the most Holy Eucharist. I adore you dwelling in the tabernacle, waiting for me to spend time with you, waiting to share yourself and your many graces with me and with all who approach you. You are the Living Bread come down from heaven; I praise you for this tremendous gift! Nourish me with your Body and your word. Increase my faith and inflame my heart with burning love for you. Remain with me and strengthen me on my pilgrim way; transform my thoughts, words, and deeds into signs of your presence for everyone whose life I touch today.

Mary Leonora Wilson, FSP

Prayer Before the Blessed Sacrament

Jesus, my Lord and my God, Creator and Ruler of the universe, I lovingly adore you, hidden so humbly beneath the appearance of the fragile Host. I am in awe to reflect that as I kneel before the Blessed Sacrament, I am not venerating a relic but worshipping the infinite God. I rejoice that the Blessed

Sacrament is not merely a holy thing but a living Person—the same Christ who died on Calvary for each and every one of us, but who loved us so much that he wanted to remain with us forever.

Dear sacramental Savior, when you rose gloriously from the tomb you showed your infinite power, but when you remain silently in the tabernacle you show your infinite love.

Like the Wise Men who worshipped you in Bethlehem under a dazzling star, I adore you under the soft glow of the sanctuary lamp during this Eucharistic hour. I cannot bring you the gifts of the Magi, but I lay at your feet my heart and soul, my very life.

Bless our Holy Father, the Pope, and the Church throughout the world. Bless those who suffer persecution for your sake, and those who preach your Gospel in distant lands. Bless our priests, our religious sisters and brothers, and increase their numbers. Bless my family and my dear departed loved ones, the sick and the homebound, those who have wandered from your fold and those who are searching for the truth.

You were my First Communion; be also the Viaticum of my old age. But in between, may you ever be my daily Bread, so that Holy Communion here on earth may be for me a sweet foretaste of an eternal union with you in heaven. Amen.

Richard Cardinal Cushing

Prayers of Praise and Thanksgiving

God doesn't need our praise or gratitude, but in offering them, our prayer is transformed.

Gratitude shifts our focus from ourselves and what we lack to God's abundant goodness. Remembering how God has loved and blessed us, we grow in faith, trusting God in all things.

Praise moves our hearts a step further, so that we focus not only on God's blessings, but also on God's very self. The Eucharist is the perfect prayer and the sacrifice of praise.

Blessed be the Father, Son, and Holy Spirit for every second that the Heart of Jesus is with us in each and every tabernacle on earth. Blessed be Emmanuel—God with us!

—Saint Manuel González García[5]

God is bread when you're hungry. God is water when you're thirsty. God is a shelter from the storm. God is rest when you're weary. God's my doctor. God's my lawyer. God's my captain who never lost a battle. God is my lily of the valley.

—Servant of God Thea Bowman

O Sacrament Most Holy

O Sacrament most holy,
     O Sacrament divine!
All praise and all thanksgiving
     be every moment thine!

May the Heart of Jesus

May the heart of Jesus in the most Blessed Sacrament be praised, adored, and loved with grateful affection at every moment, in all the tabernacles of the world, even to the end of time. Amen.

Thanks Be to Thee

Thanks be to thee, my Lord Jesus Christ,
for all the benefits
which thou hast given me,
O most merciful Friend,
Redeemer,

Brother.
May I see thee more clearly,
love thee more dearly and
follow thee more nearly.

Saint Richard of Chichester

You Have First Loved Me

I adore you, Jesus, true God and true man, present here in the Holy Eucharist. United in spirit with all the faithful on earth and all the saints in heaven, I humbly kneel before you, in deepest gratitude for so great a blessing. I love you, my Jesus, with my whole heart, for you have first loved me.

May I never offend you by my lack of love. May your Eucharistic presence completely refresh me and lead me toward heaven. Mary, Mother of our Eucharistic Lord, pray for me and obtain for me a greater love for Jesus in the Eucharist. Amen.

Filled with Wonder

O Treasure of the poor! How marvelously you sustain souls, showing the abundance of your riches to them not all at once, but little by little. When I behold your great Majesty hidden beneath so slight a Host, I am filled with wonder. . . . I know not how our Lord gives me the strength and courage necessary to draw near to him, except that he who has had, and still has, such compassion on me, gives me strength. . . . How can I open my mouth, that has uttered so many words against him, to receive that most glorious Body, purity and compassion itself? The love that is visible in his most beautiful face, sweet and tender, pains and distresses the soul because it has not served him.

Saint Teresa of Avila

Te Deum

> We praise you, O God,
> we acclaim you as Lord;
> all creation worships you,
> the Father everlasting.
> To you all angels, all the powers of heaven,
> the cherubim and seraphim, sing in
>   endless praise:
> Holy, holy, holy Lord, God of power and might,
> heaven and earth are full of your glory.

The glorious company of apostles praise you.
The noble fellowship of prophets praise you.
The white-robed army of martyrs praise you.
Throughout the world the holy Church
      acclaims you:
Father, of majesty unbounded,
your true and only Son, worthy of all praise,
the Holy Spirit, advocate and guide.
You, Christ, are the King of glory,
the eternal Son of the Father.
When you took our flesh to set us free
you humbly chose the Virgin's womb.
You overcame the sting of death
and opened the kingdom of heaven to all
      believers.
You are seated at God's right hand in glory.
We believe that you will come to be our judge.
Come then, Lord, and help your people,
bought with the price of your own Blood,
and bring us with your saints
to glory everlasting.

℣. Save your people, Lord, and bless your
      inheritance.
℟. Govern and uphold them now and always.

℣. Day by day we bless you.
℟. We praise your name forever.

℣. Keep us today, Lord, from all sin.
℟. Have mercy on us, Lord, have mercy.

℣. Lord, show us your love and mercy,
℟. for we have put our trust in you.

℣. In you, Lord, is our hope:
℟. let us never be put to shame.

Novena of Grace

We give you thanks, O Lord, for all your wondrous gifts.

We thank you for the gift of life: you called us into being so that we might be your children and live with you forever.

We thank you for our Baptism: you sealed us with the Holy Spirit, gifted us with your own life, grafted us into the Mystical Body of your divine Son.

We thank you for our vocation to join with the risen Christ in working to save and sanctify the world in which we live.

We thank you for this Eucharist: you have fed us on the Bread of Life, strengthened our faith, renewed our hope, deepened our love, made us one with one another in the Body of Christ, our Lord.

We give you thanks, O Lord, for all your wondrous gifts. Amen.

Michael Harter, SJ

A Grateful Heart

Thou hast given so much to me,
Give one thing more—a grateful heart;
Not thankful when it pleaseth me,
As if thy blessings had spare days;
But such a heart, whose pulse may be
Thy praise.

George Herbert

O Immense Love!

O my God, my true and only Love, what more could you have done to win my love? It wasn't enough for you to die for me, you instituted the Blessed Sacrament to make yourself my food, that you might give yourself entirely to me, your creature.

O immense Love! A God who gives himself totally to me! O my infinitely lovable God, I love you above all else, with all my heart. . . . In Communion you give yourself completely to me; now I give myself completely to you.

Saint Alphonsus de Liguori

Prayer of Thanksgiving

O Jesus, eternal God, thank you for your countless graces and blessings. Let every beat of my heart be a new hymn of thanksgiving to you, O God. Let every drop of my blood circulate for you, Lord. My soul is one hymn in adoration of your mercy. I love you, God, for yourself alone.

Saint Faustina Kowalska[6]

Praise of God's Love

Lord, you loved me from all eternity,
    therefore you created me.
You loved me after you had made me,
    therefore you became man for me.
You loved me after you became man for me,
    therefore you lived and died for me.
You loved me after you had died for me, therefore you rose again for me.

You loved me after you had risen for me, therefore you went to prepare a place for me.
You loved me after you had gone to prepare
a place for me, therefore you came back
to me.
You loved me after you had come back to me,
therefore you desire to enter into me
and be united with me.
This is the meaning of the Eucharist, the mystery
of love. Amen.

Alban Goodier, SJ

Litany of the Eucharist

*To make this litany even more a prayer of praise, feel free to
change the petition, "have mercy on us," to: "we praise and adore
you!"*

Lord, have mercy. ℟. *Lord, have mercy.*

Christ, have mercy. ℟. *Christ, have mercy.*

Lord, have mercy. ℟. *Lord, have mercy.*

Jesus, the Most High, ℟. *have mercy on us.*

Jesus, the holy One, ℟.

Jesus, Word of God, ℟.

Jesus, only Son of the Father, ℟.

Jesus, Son of Mary, ℟.

Jesus, crucified for us, ℟.

Jesus, risen from the dead, ℟.

Jesus, our Lord, ℟.

Jesus, our hope, ℟.

Jesus, our peace, ℟.

Jesus, our Savior, ℟.

Jesus, our salvation, ℟.

Jesus, our Resurrection, ℟.

Jesus, Lord of creation, ℟.

Jesus, lover of all, ℟.

Jesus, life of the world, ℟.

Jesus, freedom for the imprisoned, ℟.

Jesus, joy of the sorrowing, ℟.

Jesus, giver of the Spirit, ℟,.

Jesus, giver of good gifts, ℟.

Jesus, source of new life, ℟.

Jesus, Lord of Life, ℟.

Jesus, true Shepherd, ℟.

Jesus, true Light, ℟.

Jesus, Bread of heaven, ℟.

Jesus, Bread of Life, ℟.

Jesus, Bread of thaksgiving, ℟.

Jesus, life-giving Bread, ℟.

Jesus, holy manna, ℟.

Jesus, new covenant, ℟.

Jesus, food of everlasting life, ℟.

Jesus, food for our journey, ℟.

Jesus, holy banquet, ℟.

Jesus, true sacrifice, ℟.

Jesus, perfect sacrifice, ℟.

Jesus, eternal sacrifice, ℟.

Jesus, divine Victim, ℟.

Jesus, Mediator of the new Covenant, ℟.

Jesus, mystery of the altar, ℟.

Jesus, mystery of faith, ℟.

Jesus, medicine of immortality, ℟.

Jesus, pledge of eternal glory, ℟.

Jesus, Lamb of God, you take away the sins of the world, *have mercy on us.*

Jesus, Bearer of our sins, you take away the sins of the world, *have mercy on us.*

Jesus, Redeemer of the world, you take away the sins of the world, *have mercy on us.*

Christ, hear us. *Christ hear us.*

Christ, graciously hear us. *Christ, graciously hear us.*

Lord Jesus, hear our prayer. *Lord Jesus, hear our prayer.*

Prayers of Repentance and Reparation

As disciples of Christ, we are called to live in continual conversion: a demanding spiritual journey in which, recognizing the evil of sin, we daily seek to grow in self-knowledge and in heartfelt contrition for our weakness and sinful choices. Our very discomfort breaks open our hearts to receive the gifts of God's Holy Spirit. Every day we start afresh, trusting always more in God's goodness and mercy, and delighting in God's faithful love.

> The greater my unworthiness, the more abundant God's mercy.
>
> —Saint Elizabeth Ann Seton

> My God, take my heart.
> Set it on fire!
>
> —Saint Bernadette Soubirous

Act of Contrition

My God,
I am sorry for my sins with all my heart.
In choosing to do wrong
and failing to do good,
I have sinned against you
whom I should love above all things.
I firmly intend, with your help,
to do penance,
to sin no more,
and to avoid whatever leads me to sin.
Our Savior Jesus Christ
suffered and died for us.
In his name, my God, have mercy.

The Jesus Prayer

Lord Jesus Christ, Son of David,
    have mercy on me, a sinner.

Be Merciful

Be merciful, O Lord, for we have sinned.

Possess Our Hearts

Lord Jesus, our Savior,
let us now come to you.
Our hearts are cold; Lord, warm them with your
    selfless love.
Our hearts are sinful; Lord, cleanse them with
    your precious Blood.
Our hearts are weak; Lord, strengthen them with
    your joyous spirit.
Our hearts are empty; Lord, fill them with your
    divine presence.
Lord Jesus, our hearts are yours; possess them
    always and only for yourself.
Amen.

Saint Augustine

Too Late Have I Loved You

Too late have I loved you, O Beauty so ancient and so new, too late have I loved you! Behold, you were within me, while I was outside: it was there that I sought you, and, a deformed creature, rushed headlong upon these things of beauty that you have made. You were with me, but I was not with you.

They kept me far from you, those fair things which, if they were not in you, would not exist at all. You have called to me, and have cried out, and have shattered my deafness. You have blazed forth with light, and have shone upon me, and you have put my blindness to flight! You have sent forth fragrance, and I have drawn in my breath, and I pant after you. I have tasted you, and I hunger and thirst after you. You have touched me, and I have burned for your peace.

Saint Augustine[7]

Repentance and Reunion

Father, I have sinned against heaven and myself,
though you created me as your divine work.
Formed and touched by you,
my actions should have been divine.
Because I violated my own human nature,
I have also sinned before you.
Self-inflicted misery is my downfall.
I am no longer worthy of being called your child,
because I have alienated myself
of my own free will
from your creation within me—

the way you have prepared.
Now treat me as your servant,
whose freedom you paid at a high price
in the Blood of your Son.
Through Adam the inheritance of your
    children was lost to me.
But now repentance shall repay the debt of my
    sins
with the Blood of your Son.

Saint Hildegard of Bingen[8]

Litany of Repentance

For the times I have been impatient,
    ℟. *Lord, have mercy!*

For the times I have been unkind, ℟.

For the times I have acted jealously, ℟.

For my prideful boasting, ℟.

For having acted arrogantly, ℟.

For having acted dishonestly, ℟.

For those times when I have acted selfishly, ℟.

For responding irritably to others, ℟.

For my brooding over past wrongs, ℟.

For the times I rejoiced not in truth,
    but at injustice, ℟.

For the times when I gave up on others, ℟.

For my lack of faith and hope, ℟.

For setting limits to my love, ℟.

(Include other personal failings if you like.)

Marie Paul Curley, FSP

To Jesus, Good Shepherd

Jesus, you are the Good Shepherd
who gathers and cares
for the scattered sheep.
The shepherd leads
and the sheep follow
because they recognize the shepherd's voice.
You have given your commandments,
your counsels, your examples.
Whoever heeds them is nourished
with bread that does not perish:
"My food is to do the will of the heavenly Father."
Have mercy on us when we try to
nourish ourselves
on falsehood or empty pleasures.

Recall us to your way.
Sustain us when we waver, strengthen us
    when we are weak.
May everyone follow you,
Shepherd and Guardian of our souls.
You alone are the Way,
you alone have words of eternal life.
We will follow you wherever you go. Amen.

Adapted from Blessed James Alberione

Litany of the Precious Blood

Lord, have mercy. ℟. *Lord, have mercy.*

Christ, have mercy. ℟. *Christ, have mercy.*

Lord, have mercy. ℟. *Lord, have mercy.*

God our Father in heaven, ℟. *have mercy on us.*

God the Son, Redeemer of the world, ℟.

God the Holy Spirit, ℟.

Holy Trinity, one God, ℟.

Blood of Christ, only-begotten Son of
    the eternal Father, ℟. *save us.*

Blood of Christ, incarnate Word of God, ℟.

Blood of Christ, of the new and eternal covenant, ℟.

Blood of Christ, spilled upon the earth in agony, R̷.

Blood of Christ, shed freely in the scourging, R̷.

Blood of Christ, streaming forth from the crown of thorns, R̷.

Blood of Christ, poured out on the Cross, R̷.

Blood of Christ, price of our Redemption, R̷.

Blood of Christ, offering forgiveness and pardon for sin, R̷.

Blood of Christ, Eucharistic refreshment of souls, R̷.

Blood of Christ, river of mercy, R̷.

Blood of Christ, victor over evil, R̷.

Blood of Christ, strength of martyrs, R̷.

Blood of Christ, fortitude of the saints, R̷.

Blood of Christ, sustenance of virgins, R̷.

Blood of Christ, help of those in peril, R̷.

Blood of Christ, relief of the burdened, R̷.

Blood of Christ, solace in sorrow, R̷.

Blood of Christ, hope of the repentant, R̷.

Blood of Christ, consolation of the dying, R̷.

Blood of Christ, peace and comfort for hearts, R̷.

Blood of Christ, pledge of eternal life, R̷.

Blood of Christ, hope of glory, R̷.

Blood of Christ, most worthy of all honor, R̷.

Lamb of God, you take away the sins
of the world, R̷. *have mercy on us.*

Lamb of God, you take away the sins
of the world, R̷. *have mercy on us.*

Lamb of God, you take away the sins
of the world, R̷. *have mercy on us.*

V̷. You redeemed us by your Blood, O Lord.

R̷. *And made us a kingdom to serve our God.*

Let us pray.

Almighty and eternal God, you gave your Son to us to be our Redeemer. Grant that his saving Blood be a safeguard against every evil, so that we may rejoice in its fruits forever in heaven. Through the same Christ our Lord. Amen.

Angel of Fatima's Prayers of Reparation

Most Holy Trinity, Father, Son and Holy Spirit, I adore you profoundly, and I offer you the most precious Body, Blood, soul, and divinity of Jesus Christ, present in all the tabernacles of the world, in reparation for the outrages, sacrileges, and indifference by which he is offended. By the infinite merits of the Sacred Heart of Jesus, and the Immaculate Heart of Mary, I beg of you the conversion of poor sinners.

O my Jesus, forgive us our sins, save us from the fires of hell, lead all souls to heaven, especially those most in need of thy mercy.

My God, I believe, I adore, I trust, and I love thee! I beg pardon for all those that do not believe, do not adore, do not trust, and do not love thee.

Most Holy Trinity, I adore thee! My God, I love thee in the most Blessed Sacrament.

Litany of Reparation to the Most Holy Sacrament

Lord, have mercy on us.

℟. *Christ, have mercy on us.*

Lord, have mercy on us. Christ, hear us.

℟. *Christ, graciously hear us.*

God the Father of heaven, ℟. *have mercy on us.*

God the Son, Redeemer of the world, ℟.

God the Holy Spirit, ℟.

Holy Trinity, one God, ℟.

Sacred Host, offered for the salvation of sinners, ℟.

Sacred Host, humbled at the altar for us and by us, ℟.

Sacred Host, despised and neglected, ℟.

Sacred Host, sign of contradiction, ℟.

Sacred Host, insulted by blasphemers, ℟.

Sacred Host, dishonored by unfaithful ministers, ℟.

Sacred Host, received without love or devotion, ℟.

Sacred Host, forgotten and abandoned in your
  churches, ℟.

O God, be favorable to us and pardon us. ℟.

O Lord, be favorable to us and hear us. ℟.

For so many unworthy Communions, Lord,
  ℟. *we offer you our reparation.*

For the irreverence of Christians, ℟.

For the unbelief of Catholics, ℟.

For the desecration of your sanctuaries, ℟.

For the holy vessels dishonored and stolen, ℟.

For the blasphemies of the wicked, ℟.

For unworthy conversations carried on in your
  churches, ℟.

For the sacrileges which profane your Sacrament
  of love, ℟.

For the indifference of so many of your children, ℟.

For the contempt of your loving invitations, ℟.

For the abuse of your grace, ℟.

For our unfaithfulness and infidelity toward you in the most Holy Sacrament, ℟.

For our lukewarmness in loving and serving you, ℟.

For the rejection of those who have left you, ℟.

For your immense sorrow at the loss of souls, ℟.

For an increase in respect towards this adorable Mystery in all Christians, ℟. *we beseech you, hear us.*

That you manifest the Sacrament of your love to unbelievers, ℟.

That you give us grace to love you in reparation for those who hate you, ℟.

That you cast upon us the injuries of those who outrage you, ℟.

That you receive our humble reparation, ℟.

That our adoration may be pleasing to you, ℟.

Sacred Host, ℟. *hear us.*

Holy Host, ℟. *graciously hear us.*

Lamb of God, who takes away the sins of the world, ℟. *pardon us.*

Lamb of God, who takes away the sins of the world,
℟. *hear us.*

Lamb of God, who takes away the sins of the world,
℟. *have mercy on us.*

Let us pray.

Lord Jesus Christ, who are pleased to dwell with us in your wonderful Sacrament until the end of time, and by this memory of your passion to render to your Father eternal glory and bestow on us the food of immortality, grant us the grace to mourn with hearts filled with sorrow the many injuries you receive in this adorable Mystery, and the numberless sacrileges committed. Inflame us with an ardent zeal to repair all the insults to which you have preferred to expose yourself, rather than deprive us of your Presence and be separated from us. May we never cease to love and praise you who, with God the Father and the Holy Spirit, live and reign, God, forever and ever. Amen.

Act of Reparation to the Most Blessed Sacrament

Eucharistic Jesus,
kneeling before you, I adore you,
hidden in the most holy Sacrament of the altar,

and with my whole heart I love you.
In reparation for all the offences,
profanations, and sacrileges,
committed by myself or others against you,
or that may be committed in times to come,
I offer to you, my God,
my humble adoration,
not indeed as you deserve,
nor as much as I desire,
but as far as I am able;
wishing that I could love you
with the most perfect love possible.
I offer you all the discomfort, sorrow, and pain
    that comes my way
in reparation for the insults, neglect,
    and rejection you endure
in this Sacrament, where you remain for love
    of us.
I desire to adore you now and always,
for all those who do not adore or love you.
Yes, my Jesus, may you be known,
adored, and loved by everyone,
and may thanks be continually given to you
in this most holy Sacrament! Amen.

Mary Leonora Wilson, FSP

Stations of the Cross

You can pray the Way of the Cross following the images in your church, moving from station to station, or, if that is not possible, by simply gazing at a crucifix and calling to mind each individual station. Either way, what is important is to contemplate the great love of Jesus for you and for humanity in undergoing so much suffering and offering his life for our salvation. We suggest that as you accompany Jesus along his sorrowful road to Calvary, you:

— Begin each station with the prayer:

> We adore you, O Christ,
> > and we bless you,
> because by your holy Cross
> > you have redeemed the world.

— Call to mind the station with its Scripture prompt and reflect on it.

— Offer a brief prayer or aspiration (one is provided for those who wish).

— End each station, joining yourself to Mary most holy, with the prayer:

Holy Mother! Pierce me through;
In my heart each wound renew
Of my Savior crucified.

— Proceed to the next station.

I Station

Jesus is condemned to death

He was oppressed, and he was afflicted,
  yet he did not open his mouth;
like a lamb that is led to the slaughter (Is 53:7).

Jesus Master, you accept the bitter chalice of death for love of us! You are my example and my strength.

II Station

Jesus takes up his Cross

We have all turned to our own way,
and the Lord has laid on him
  the iniquity of us all (Is 53:6).

Lord Jesus, I adore your divine love and fortitude. Teach me to respond in love, embracing the Cross when it comes my way.

III Station

Jesus falls the first time

I am ready to fall,
and my pain is ever with me (Ps 38:17).

Blessed Jesus, even in apparent powerlessness you are redeeming us! Each time I fall may I draw closer to you in trust.

IV Station

Jesus meets his afflicted mother

A sword will pierce your soul (see Lk 2:35).

Most Sorrowful Mother, you never abandon your divine Son but remain at his side always. Teach me to love as you love.

V Station

Simon of Cyrene helps Jesus carry the Cross

If any want to become my followers, let them deny themselves and take up their cross and follow me (Mk 8:34).

Loving Redeemer, Simon's life was changed by this act of compassion. Accept my offering of love and allow me to lift some of the weight from your rejected Heart.

VI Station

Veronica wipes the face of Jesus

I looked for pity, but there was none;
> and for comforters, but I found none
> (Ps 69:20).

Suffering Jesus, how your face has been disfigured by the tortures you endured! Like Veronica, grant me the grace to recognize your face in everyone I meet.

VII Station

Jesus falls the second time

My soul clings to the dust (Ps 119:25).

Lord Jesus Christ, our repeated sins and indifference thrust you to the ground once again. As much as I have offended you, now let me love and adore you even more!

VIII Station

Jesus comforts the women of Jerusalem

The joy of our hearts has ceased;
> our dancing has been turned to mourning
> > (Lam 5:15).

Merciful Lord, even in your extreme suffering your first thought is for others. Impress the charity of your Heart on my heart!

IX Station

Jesus falls the third time

I am utterly spent and crushed (Ps 38:8).

Divine Savior, insults are heaped upon you as you fall again. Let me atone for these by lifting you up in those who are suffering and by offering you adoration and praise.

X Station

Jesus is stripped of his garments

He was despised and rejected by others;
>   a man of suffering . . .
one from whom others hide their faces;
>   he was despised, and we held him of no
>   account (Is 53:3).

Meek Redeemer, how cruelly you are stripped, and your wounded body exposed! While I weep for those who deride you, let me learn from your forgiveness and compassion.

XI Station

Jesus is nailed to the Cross

They have pierced my hands and my feet;
I can count all my bones.
They stare and gloat over me (see Ps 22:16–17).

Crucified Lord, nailed to the altar of the Cross, slain to ransom us from the grip of Satan! Let my heart never turn away from you again.

XII Station

Jesus dies on the Cross

"Father, into your hands I commend my spirit"
  (Lk 23:46).

Jesus, Son of God, your sacrifice is complete; you, the Innocent One were immolated to redeem us from our sins. Make my love for you strong and capable of the ultimate sacrifice.

XIII Station

Jesus is taken down from the Cross

Even though I walk through the darkest valley,
    I fear no evil;
for you are with me (Ps 23:4).

Silent Lord, for a brief time death would seem to claim you, but you have conquered death and won eternal life for us. Let me always live for you—now and eternally!

XIV Station

Jesus is laid in the tomb

Weeping may linger for the night,
but joy comes with the morning (Ps 30:5).

Immortal God, once concealed in the tomb; now concealed under the appearance of bread in our tabernacles. May I keep vigil in adoration before you until I behold your face forever in eternal life.

To Jesus Crucified

Good and gentle Jesus, I kneel before you and with fervent desire ask that you fill my heart with sentiments of faith, hope, and love, repentance for my sins, and true conversion of life.

As I see and contemplate your five precious wounds, I recall the words that David prophesied long ago, my Jesus: "They have pierced my hands and my feet; I can count all my bones" (see Ps 22:17–18).

To conclude the Stations, pray one Our Father, one Hail Mary, and one Glory to the Father for the intentions of the Holy Father.

The Sacrament of Reconciliation

In the sacrament of Reconciliation (also called Penance or confession), we present ourselves contrite before God, who showers his healing grace on our souls. It is a wonderful preparation for receiving Holy Communion. Through this sacrament, God repairs and strengthens our baptismal bonds both with himself and with the Church. Confession brings us to Christ, who fills us with life. Because going to confession can powerfully change us, it's the last thing the devil wants. So we can expect many barriers and obstacles and much emotional resistance to the sacrament. We should go anyway. Jesus wants to meet us in this sacrament and fill us with life so that we may be strengthened against the temptations of Satan and prepared for death and judgment.

While preparing for confession, ask God to help you see and accept the particular sins for which you are responsible. Then explore your behavior since your last confession. One way to jog your mind and heart is through reflection on the Ten Commandments, which helps you focus your thoughts and look over your life.

After confession, a crown is given to penitents!

—Saint Alphonsus de Liguori,
quoting Saint John Chrysostom

Celebrating the Sacrament of Reconciliation

Reflect and understand clearly how your behavior has damaged your relationship with God, the Church, and people in your life.

Begin with a Sign of the Cross and tell the priest how long it has been since your last confession.

Tell the priest your sins.

Listen for any words from him that may help you to deepen your faithfulness to Christ and to avoid repeating the sins.

When the priest gives you a penance, indicate you understand it, or ask for clarification if you don't.

Say an Act of Contrition (see page 70).

Listen to the words of absolution.

Complete your penance.

Thank God for this great moment of grace in your life.

Counsels for Living a Christian Life

THE TEN COMMANDMENTS
See Exodus 20:1–17

I am the Lord your God:
>   You shall not have other gods besides me.
>   You shall not take the name of the Lord
>   your God in vain.
>   Remember to keep holy the Lord's day.
>   Honor your father and your mother.
>   You shall not kill.
>   You shall not commit adultery.
>   You shall not steal.
>   You shall not bear false witness against
>   your neighbor.
>   You shall not covet your neighbor's wife.
>   You shall not covet your neighbor's goods.

The Beatitudes
Matthew 5:3–12

Blessed are the poor in spirit, for theirs is the kingdom of heaven.

Blessed are those who mourn, for they will be comforted.

Blessed are the meek, for they will inherit the earth.

Blessed are those who hunger and thirst for righteousness, for they will be filled.

Blessed are the merciful, for they will receive mercy.

Blessed are the pure in heart, for they will see God.

Blessed are the peacemakers, for they will be called children of God.

Blessed are those who are persecuted for righteousness' sake, for theirs is the kingdom of heaven.

Blessed are you when people revile you and persecute you and utter all kinds of evil against you falsely on my account. Rejoice and be glad, for your reward is great in heaven, for in the same way they persecuted the prophets who were before you.

Prayers of Intercession and Petition

Asking God for what we need is perhaps the most instinctive prayer we humans can make. God delights when we turn to him in trust, whether our petition is for something great or small. Above all, we pray for the coming of the kingdom of God, for personal transformation in Christ, and for the graces we need to be Christ for others.

True Eucharistic prayer is intercessory: we bring not just ourselves and our own concerns to Jesus in the Eucharist, but also the urgent needs of others from all over the world.

> Be "big-hearted" enough in prayer to embrace everyone in the world.
>
> —Venerable Thecla Merlo, FSP

When we leave Mass, we ought to go out the way Moses descended Mount Sinai: with his face shining, with his heart brave and strong to face the world's difficulties.

—Saint Oscar Romero[9]

As I Walk in Your Light

Jesus in the Eucharist,
give me the grace of a cheerful heart,
an even temper, sweetness,
gentleness, and brightness of mind
as I walk in your light and by your grace.
I pray you to give me the spirit
of over-abundant, ever-springing love,
which overpowers the vexations of life
by its own riches and strength
and which, above all things, unites me to you
who are the fountain and the center of all mercy,
    loving kindness, and joy. Amen.

Saint John Henry Newman

God's Dream for Me

Your dream, O Master, is to lay hold of me with
    your divine life.

Your dream is to purify me, to recreate me, to
make me a new person in your image.

Your dream is to fill me with your love, so that I
love the Father and all my brothers and
sisters just as you do.

Your dream is to draw me to you with the closest
bonds,
to unite my heart with yours, to make me strong,
to impart to me your divine power so that I can
overcome evil and be constant in doing good.

Your dream is to inflame me with untiring zeal
to spread your kingdom.
Your dream is to possess me in this life and in
the life to come.
May your dream come true! May I be able to give
all you ask of me. Amen.

Adapted from Blessed James Alberione

For Faith in the Real Presence

I come to you, Lord, like the Apostles, to pray,
"Increase my faith." Give me a strong and lively faith
that you are really present in the Eucharist; an active
faith that will direct my life.

Give me the remarkable faith of the centurion, which drew forth such praise from you. Give me the faith of the beloved disciple to recognize you and exclaim, "It is the Lord!" Give me the faith of Peter to confess, "You are the Christ, Son of the living God!" Give me the faith of Mary Magdalen to bow down at your feet and cry out, "Rabboni! Master!"

Give me the faith of all the saints to whom the Eucharist was heaven begun here on earth. Each time I receive the Eucharist and each time I make a visit to the Blessed Sacrament, increase my faith and love, my humility and reverence, and my trust that all good things will come to me.

My Lord and my God, increase my faith!

Prayer for the Gifts of the Holy Spirit

Divine Holy Spirit,
eternal Love of the Father and of the Son,
I adore you, I thank you, I love you,
and I ask your forgiveness
for all the times I have sinned against you
and against my neighbor.
Descend with many graces
on those ordained as bishops and priests,

on those consecrated as men and women religious,
on those who receive the sacrament of
    Confirmation.
Be light, sanctity, and zeal for them.
To you, Spirit of truth,
I dedicate my mind, imagination, and memory.
Enlighten me.
Bring me to fuller knowledge of Jesus Christ,
and a deeper understanding of the Gospel and
    the teaching of the Church.
Increase in me the gifts of wisdom, knowledge,
    understanding, and counsel.
To you, sanctifying Spirit,
I dedicate my will.
Guide me, make me faithful in living fully
the commandments and my vocation.
Grant me the gifts of fortitude and holy fear
    of God.
To you, life-giving Spirit,
I dedicate my heart.
Guard me from evil; pour on me an always
    greater abundance of your life.
Bring to completion your work in me.
Grant me the gift of piety. Amen.

Blessed James Alberione

To My Guardian Angel, Companion in Adoration

My Guardian Angel, with your companion angels you constantly behold the face of God. You were created to adore, glorify, and praise the Divine Trinity. Even while helping me in my earthly pilgrimage, you remain always united with God, immersed in his presence and his holiness, beholding his beauty, and radiating his love. Teach me, O blessed companion, to adore the Lord present in the most holy Sacrament of the Eucharist, inspired by your own great love and singleness of heart. Like you, I too have been created to adore, love, and serve God, my Creator and Redeemer. Unlike you, my vision is often obscured by distractions or spiritual darkness. Help me then, dear angel, to pray always, to keep my gaze fixed on Jesus, to walk before the Father with humility, gratitude, and trust. May my life be a living sacrifice of praise and may the fire of adoration always burn lovingly in my heart. With you, I pray:

"Blessing and glory and wisdom
and thanksgiving and honor

and power and might
be to our God forever and ever!" (Rev 7:12)

Mary Leonora Wilson, FSP

Act of Trust in the Divine Master

The Master is here and is calling you (see Jn 11:28).

The Master is here in my personal story with its lights and shadows. Jesus is calling me to accept my story as he does and to explore the vast horizons of his peace.

The Master is here in my work and in my service.

The Master is here in my family and my community. He is calling me to communicate with them, to trust and to live his love.

The Master is here in the Church, in its efforts for evangelization and service, in the liturgy, which pulsates with the power of the Holy Spirit. Jesus is calling me to contemplate his mysteries as they unfold throughout the liturgical year.

The Master is here in the poor and the oppressed, in those who suffer or have lost their way, in those who need the light of my faith and the gift of my love.

The Master is here in the depths of my heart. He is calling me to open the door to him so that he might dwell within me, his chosen home.

Giovannamaria Carrara, FSP

Heart of Love

O Heart of love,
I place my trust entirely in you.
Though I fear all things from my weakness,
I hope all things from your goodness!

Saint Margaret Mary Alacoque

Prayer of Saint Francis

Lord, make me an instrument of your peace:
where there is hatred, let me sow love;
where there is discord, harmony;
where there is injury, pardon;
where there is error, truth;
where there is doubt, faith;
where there is despair, hope;
where there is darkness, light;
where there is sadness, joy.

Divine Master, grant that I may not so much seek
to be consoled as to console;

to be understood, as to understand;
to be loved, as to love.
For it is in giving that we receive;
it is in forgetting self that we find ourselves;
it is in pardoning that we are pardoned;
and it is in dying that we are born to eternal life.

Prayer of Surrender

Father, I abandon myself into your hands;
do with me what you will.
Whatever you may do, I thank you;
I am ready for all, I accept all.
Let only your will be done in me,
and in all your creatures.
I wish no more than this, O Lord.
Into your hands I commend myself;
I offer myself to you with all the love of my heart,
for I love you, Lord, and so need to give myself,
to surrender myself into your hands without
    reserve,
and with boundless confidence, for you are my
    Father.

Saint Charles de Foucauld

Shine Through Me

Dear Jesus, help me to spread your fragrance everywhere I go. Flood my soul with your Spirit and life. Penetrate and possess my whole being so utterly that my life may only be a radiance of yours.

Shine through me and be so in me that every person I come in contact with may feel your presence in my soul. Let them look up, and see no longer me, but only Jesus! Stay with me and then I shall begin to shine as you shine, shining so as to be a light to others. The light, Jesus, will be all from you; none of it will be mine. It will be you shining on others through me. Let me thus praise you in the way that you love best, by shining on those around me.

Let me preach you without preaching, not by my words but by my example, by the catching force, the sympathetic influence of what I do, the evident fullness of the love my heart bears for you. Amen.

Saint John Henry Newman

Soul of Jesus

Soul of Jesus, sanctify me.
Blood of Jesus, wash me.
Passion of Jesus, comfort me.

Wounds of Jesus, hide me.

Heart of Jesus, receive me.

Spirit of Jesus, enliven me.

Goodness of Jesus, pardon me.

Beauty of Jesus, draw me.

Humility of Jesus, humble me.

Peace of Jesus, pacify me.

Love of Jesus, inflame me.

Kingdom of Jesus, come to me.

Grace of Jesus, replenish me.

Mercy of Jesus, pity me.

Sanctity of Jesus, sanctify me.

Purity of Jesus, purify me.

Cross of Jesus, support me.

Nails of Jesus, hold me.

Mouth of Jesus, bless me in life, defend me in the hour of death.

Mouth of Jesus, call me to come to you
and receive me with your saints in glory evermore.

Let us pray.

Unite me to you, O adorable Jesus. Life-giving heavenly Bread, feed me, sanctify me, reign in me, transform me into yourself; live in me and let me live in you; let me adore you in your life-giving Sacrament as my God, listen to you as to my Master, obey you as my King, imitate you as my Model, follow you as my Shepherd, love you as my Father, seek you as my Physician who heals all the maladies of my soul. Be indeed my Way, Truth, and Life; sustain me, O heavenly Manna, through the desert of this world, till I shall behold you unveiled in glory. Amen.

Saint Elizabeth Ann Seton

Come, Holy Spirit

Come, Holy Spirit, fill the hearts of your faithful
and enkindle in them the fire of your love.
Send forth your Spirit and they shall be created,
and you shall renew the face of the earth.

For Protection and Enlightenment

May the strength of God pilot us.
May the power of God preserve us.
May the wisdom of God instruct us.
May the hand of God protect us.
May the way of God direct us.
May the shield of God defend us.
May the hosts of God protect us.
Now and always.

Saint Patrick

Prayer for the Needs of Others

God of love, whose compassion never fails,
we bring you the sufferings of the world,
the needs of the homeless,
the cries of prisoners,
the pains of the sick and injured,
the sorrow of the bereaved,
the helplessness of the elderly and weak.
According to their needs and your great mercy,
strengthen and relieve them
in Jesus Christ our Lord.

Saint Anselm

In Our Daily Living

Lord of the world and of peace,
help us to unite these two words
in our daily life.
Peace in the world and peace in our hearts—
this we ask of you, Lord,
for if there is to be peace in the world,
there must be peace in our hearts.
Remove from us hate and rancor
and everything that impedes

a serene and happy way of life.
Give us your peace, O Lord,
the peace that the world often
does not understand or value,
but without which,
the world cannot live.

Gloria Bordeghini, FSP

Prayer for Priests

Jesus, eternal High Priest,
bless all priests so that they may fulfill their
    priestly vocation:
to believe profoundly,
to profess their faith with courage,
to pray fervently,
to teach with deep conviction, to serve,
to put into practice in their own lives
the program of the beatitudes,
to know how to love disinterestedly,
to be close to everyone,
especially those who are most in need.

Adapted from Saint John Paul II[10]

To Foster Respect for Life

O Mary, bright dawn of the new world,
Mother of the living, to you do we entrust the
    cause of life:
Look down, O Mother, upon the vast
    numbers
of babies not allowed to be born,
of the poor whose lives are made difficult,
of men and women who are victims of brutal
    violence,
of the elderly and the sick killed by indifference
    or out of misguided mercy.
Grant that all who believe in your Son
may proclaim the Gospel of life with honesty
    and love
to the people of our time.
Obtain for them the grace to accept that Gospel
    as a gift ever new,
the joy of celebrating it with gratitude through-
    out their lives,
and the courage to bear witness to it resolutely,
in order to build, together with all people of
    goodwill,

the civilization of truth and love,
to the praise and glory of God,
the Creator and lover of life.

Saint John Paul II[11]

Prayer of Saint Gertrude for the Souls in Purgatory

Eternal Father, in union with the Masses said throughout the world today, I offer you the most precious Blood of your divine Son, Jesus, for all the holy souls in purgatory, for sinners everywhere, for sinners in the universal Church, for those in my own home and within my family. Amen.

Saint Gertrude

Divine Mercy Chaplet

The Divine Mercy Chaplet is prayed on an ordinary five-decade rosary.

Begin with an Our Father, Hail Mary, and Apostles' Creed.

On the single bead before each decade:

Eternal Father, I offer you the Body and Blood, soul and divinity of your dearly beloved Son, our

Lord Jesus Christ, in atonement for our sins and those of the whole world.

On the ten beads of each decade:

For the sake of his sorrowful passion, have mercy on us and on the whole world.

After the five decades, conclude with:

Holy God, Holy Mighty One, Holy Immortal One, have mercy on us and on the whole world (*three times*).

Saint Faustina Kowalska

Invocations to the Eucharistic Heart of Jesus

In the following invocations, we confidently remind Jesus of the Promises of his own Sacred Heart made to Saint Margaret Mary Alacoque.

Eucharistic Heart of Jesus, grant peace to our families: *We trust in your promise.*

Eucharistic Heart of Jesus, grant us all the graces necessary for our state of life: *We trust in your promise.*

Eucharistic Heart of Jesus, console us in our suffering: *We trust in your promise.*

Eucharistic Heart of Jesus, be our safe shelter in each troubled hour of our life: *We trust in your promise.*

Eucharistic Heart of Jesus, be our refuge in the moment of death: *We trust in your promise.*

Eucharistic Heart of Jesus, abundantly bless all our undertakings: *We trust in your promise.*

Eucharistic Heart of Jesus, be the source and ocean of mercy for all of us sinners: *We trust in your promise.*

Eucharistic Heart of Jesus, change the lukewarm into your fervent lovers: *We trust in your promise.*

Eucharistic Heart of Jesus, let the fervent rise quickly to great perfection: *We trust in your promise.*

Eucharistic Heart of Jesus, bless the places and houses where your image is displayed and honored: *We trust in your promise.*

Eucharistic Heart of Jesus, give priests the power to move the most hardened hearts: *We trust in your promise.*

Eucharistic Heart of Jesus, write on your Heart the names of those who spread your devotion: *We trust in your promise.*

Eucharistic Heart of Jesus, grant the grace of everlasting life to those who, for nine months and with sentiments of reparation, receive Communion on the First Friday: *We trust in your promise.*

Eucharistic Heart of Jesus, refresh all those who come to you oppressed and weary: *We trust in your promise.*

Eucharistic Heart of Jesus, grant us all the graces that we ask of the Father in your name: *We trust in your promise.*

Eucharistic Heart of Jesus, send good workers into your harvest: *We trust in your promise.*

Eucharistic Heart of Jesus, grant goodwill to all who ask it of you: *We trust in your promise.*

Eucharistic Heart of Jesus, grant us the gift of wisdom: *We trust in your promise.*

Eucharistic Heart of Jesus, grant the Church perpetual triumph over hell: *We trust in your promise.*

Eucharistic Heart of Jesus, give the living water of holiness to whoever asks for it: *We trust in your promise.*

Eucharistic Heart of Jesus, remain always with your apostles of the word and the pen: *We trust in your promise.*

Eucharistic Heart of Jesus, be with the family that prays together: *We trust in your promise.*

Eucharistic Heart of Jesus, always hear our prayers in life and in death: *We trust in your promise.*

Let us pray.

Father, in the death and Resurrection of your Son you redeemed all people. Guard your work of mercy in us so that, in assiduous celebration of the paschal mystery, we will receive the fruits of our salvation. Through Christ our Lord. Amen.

Blessed James Alberione

In Adoration with Mary

Many saints eloquently encourage us to follow their example of making Mary our way to Jesus. Saint Peter Julian Eymard puts it well:

> Where shall we find Jesus on earth if not in Mary's arms? Did she not give us the Eucharist? Was it not her consent to the Incarnation of the Word in her pure womb that inaugurated the great mystery of reparation to God and union with us, which Jesus accomplished by his mortal life, and that he continues in the Eucharist?
>
> Without Mary, we shall not find Jesus, for she possesses him in her Heart. There he takes his delight, and those who wish to know his inmost virtues, his sacred and privileged love, must seek them in the Heart of Mary. Those who love that good Mother will find Jesus in her pure Heart.
>
> We must never separate Jesus from Mary. We can go to him only through her.[12]

Three compelling reasons for going to Jesus through Mary are:

1. From the Cross, Jesus gave us Mary as our Mother;
2. God chose Mary to be his own Mother;
3. Mary was the first adorer of her Son and his first and closest disciple.

In praying to Mary, we entrust ourselves to her motherly care, as Jesus invites us. "Behold your mother!" (see Jn 19:27)

Look up at the star, call on Mary! With her for a guide, you will never go astray.

— Saint Bernard of Clairvaux

Like a branch ever bearing its fruit and offering it to everyone, Mary always gives Jesus: suffering, glorious, Eucharistic, the Way, Truth, and Life of humanity.

— Blessed James Alberione

The Mysteries of the Rosary: Eucharistic Reflections

THE JOYFUL MYSTERIES

Usually prayed on Mondays and Saturdays

In these Joyful Mysteries, we meditate on the reality of Jesus Christ's presence among us in the Holy Eucharist. Each mystery has a Eucharistic reflection and the option of praying for the grace to imitate a particular Eucharistic virtue.

1. The Annunciation to the Blessed Virgin Mary (Lk 1:26–38)

The archangel Gabriel announces to Mary the coming of the Savior and Mary's divine motherhood. At her assent, the Son of God "empties himself" of the trappings of divinity and is conceived by the Virgin Mary, who lovingly receives him and adores him as his handmaid. Mary becomes the first tabernacle of the Word made flesh, his first and most perfect adorer.

Eucharistic virtue: *Humility*

2. Mary Visits Her Cousin Elizabeth (Lk 1:39–45)

In Mary's visit, Saint Elizabeth recognizes the presence of her Lord: "How is it that the mother of my Lord should come to *me*?" (see Lk. 1:43). In the Holy Eucharist, Jesus is really, truly present in our midst, even though hidden under ordinary appearances. Joyful recognition, thanksgiving, and praise are the most appropriate responses we can give at every Eucharistic encounter.

When we receive the Lord as Mary did, we become *living* tabernacles, who bring Jesus to others wherever we go.

Eucharistic virtue: *Love for one's neighbor*

3. The Birth of Jesus at Bethlehem (Lk 2:1–7)

The Incarnation and the Eucharist, two of the greatest mysteries of our faith, are astonishing expressions of God's love for us. Out of love for us, our humble God becomes a baby, drawing unimaginably close to us, making himself vulnerable to sinful human beings. Hiding his divinity so that he can be in our midst seems to us to be beneath his divine dignity, but not to God! How lovable as a tiny Infant!

And how infinitely lovable even more in his humble presence in the Eucharist!

Eucharistic virtue: *Poverty of spirit*

4. The Presentation of Jesus in the Temple (Lk 2:22–24)

Mary and Joseph present Jesus in the Temple, fulfilling the Law and offering him back to the Father. Mary and Joseph were not only consecrating Jesus to fulfill his divine mission but were saying a wholehearted "yes" to participating in that mission—a participation in which Mary would sacrifice her Heart as Jesus would sacrifice his life.

Like Mary, we too are called to participate in Jesus' sacrifice on the Cross, an oblation that Jesus renews in every Eucharist. With him, we offer ourselves to the Father in all our joys and sufferings.

Eucharistic virtue: *Spirit of loving sacrifice*

5. The Finding of the Child Jesus in the Temple (Lk 2:41–51)

After three frantic days of searching, Mary and Joseph find twelve-year-old Jesus teaching in the Temple. Jesus is found . . . but he was never truly lost: "I must be in my Father's house." Mary and Joseph surely felt that *they* were the ones who were lost during those three dark days as they sought Jesus with anguished longing. When we feel like we have lost Jesus or are longing for the peace, joy, and fulfillment that only God can give, let us go to the tabernacle! We will always *be found* in his Eucharistic presence.

Eucharistic virtue: *Longing for the Bread of Life*

THE LUMINOUS MYSTERIES
Usually prayed on Thursdays

In these Luminous Mysteries, we meditate on the reality of Jesus Christ's saving work among us and for us.

1. John Baptizes Jesus in the Jordan (Mt 3:13–17)

When John the Baptist baptizes Jesus, the Father affirms Jesus' identity as his Beloved Son. In his life, death, and Resurrection, Jesus won for us the privilege of becoming God's cherished sons and daughters, an identity we received at our Baptism that can never be taken away. Every time we encounter Jesus in the Eucharist, Jesus affirms, nurtures, and deepens our identity as God's beloved ones.

Eucharistic virtue: *Gratitude for our identity as beloved in Christ*

2. Jesus Reveals His Glory at the Wedding of Cana (Jn 2:1–11)

At Mary's request, Jesus turns water into wine, providing an abundance of wine for the wedding feast. This miracle, containing so many Eucharistic allusions, comes about because Mary so confidently trusts in her Son's saving mission.

Mary's request to Jesus launches his public ministry and helps the disciples to begin to see who Jesus truly is. Mary always leads us to Jesus; she encourages us to open our hearts to faith in his saving work in our lives: "Do whatever he tells you" (Jn. 2:5). She is the one who can best help us to live a truly Eucharistic life.

Eucharistic virtue: *Confident trust in Jesus*

3. Jesus Proclaims the Kingdom of God and Calls Us to Conversion (Mk 1:14–15)

Jesus invites all to enter the kingdom of God with the words, "Repent, and believe in the good news" (Mk. 1:15). We begin every Mass expressing our sorrow for our sins. Frequently receiving the Sacrament of Penance delights the Lord and removes any obstacles to Jesus bringing about the kingdom of God more fully in us when we receive him in Holy Communion. No one is ever truly worthy to receive our Eucharistic Lord, but we *can* prepare our hearts to be a place of joy and consolation for him.

Eucharistic virtue: *Spirit of repentance and reparation*

4. The Transfiguration of Jesus (Lk 9:28–36)

On Mount Tabor when Jesus is transfigured before the three apostles, they wanted to remain and bask in the radiance of his glory. This glorious moment of light was meant to strengthen the apostles during Christ's upcoming passion and death. In the presence of the hidden glory of the Eucharistic Jesus, as we bask in the light of his tender and victorious love, we can ask Jesus for the gift to unite our moments of darkness and pain with his self-offering to the Father.

Eucharistic virtue: *Fortitude*

5. Jesus Gives Us the Eucharist (Jn 6:22–65)

On the night he was betrayed, Jesus gave us the unsurpassable gift of his very self in the Holy Eucharist, to make present to us for all time the sacrifice of the Cross that he offered to the Father for our salvation on Calvary: "Before the festival of the Passover, Jesus knew that his hour had come to depart from this world and go to the Father. Having loved his own who were in the world, he loved them to the end" (Jn. 13:1).

Jesus gives himself to us in love in the Holy Eucharist to enable us to live his last request, "Abide in my love" (Jn 15:9).

Eucharistic virtue: *Union with Christ*

THE SORROWFUL MYSTERIES

Usually prayed on Tuesdays and Fridays

In the Sorrowful Mysteries, we meditate on the tremendous love of the Lord for us and the urgency for us to respond to him in love and reparation. An option to offer reparatory intentions with each decade is suggested.

1. Jesus Prays in the Garden of Gethsemane (Lk 22:39–46)

Jesus is overcome with anguish and dread over the sufferings he is about to face: especially the devastating weight of the sins of all humanity, which he is taking on himself. He first turns to the Father in prayer but then seeks out his chosen apostles, who, instead of waiting up with him, abandon him by falling asleep. "Could you not watch one hour with me?" was his desolate cry in the Garden of Gethsemane, but how many times has Jesus repeated it from the tabernacles in the empty churches where he is always available?

Reparatory intention: *In reparation for the times when Jesus in the Holy Eucharist has been ignored, neglected, or abandoned.*

2. Jesus Is Scourged at the Pillar (Jn 19:1)

After his arrest and mock trial, the most sacred Body of Christ, from whom so many had found healing, is most cruelly scourged. His sacred Blood freely soaks into the ground. Yet the Son of God humbly submits to this heinous torture. How can we give greater reverence and adoration to Christ's same sacred Body and Blood present on every altar, in every tabernacle?

Reparatory intention: *In reparation for the sacrileges, blasphemies, or other acts of disrespect committed against Jesus in the most Blessed Sacrament.*

3. Jesus Is Crowned with Thorns (Mk 15:16–20)

The Word of Life, the One who *is* Truth, is ridiculed and mocked as a false king and crowned with thorns. Jesus remains silent against this gratuitous brutality. He remains defenseless like all the poor ones of this world who have no protection against misunderstanding, derision, or savagely callous abuse. Jesus' Eucharistic littleness reminds us how precious the "little ones" of the world are to him.

Reparatory intention: *In reparation for those who mock the Eucharist and the love of Christ, for those who mock Christ present in others, and for those who have rejected the gift of faith that they have received.*

4. Jesus Carries the Cross to Calvary (Jn 19:17)

Jesus takes the Cross upon his shoulders, but as heavy as the wood of the Cross was, heavier by far to bear is the evil of the sins of all humanity. Each excruciating step Jesus takes must have felt beyond his strength, but he keeps going. Every step of Jesus' way of the Cross is an act of unprecedented love and fidelity for the Father and for you: a faithful love you behold every time you encounter him in the Eucharist, and a faithful love that he calls you to imitate.

Reparatory intention: *In reparation for those who, out of weakness or human respect, make poor Communions, receive Jesus while in the state of grievous sin, or miss going to Mass on Sundays.*

5. Jesus Dies for Our Sins (Jn 19:30)

At every Mass, Jesus offers himself in that same sacrifice to the Father on our behalf. The Eucharist is a mystery of love beyond words, beyond our comprehension. Jesus explains what he wants us to understand and live by his passion and death: "No one has greater love than this, to lay down one's life for one's friends. You are my friends if you do what I command you" (Jn 15:13–14).

Reparatory intention: *In reparation for our own sins, the sins of family and friends, and the sins of those souls who are called to a greater life of love, especially devout laity, bishops and priests, religious brothers and sisters.*

THE GLORIOUS MYSTERIES

Usually prayed on Wednesdays and Sundays

In the Glorious Mysteries of the Rosary, we contemplate with gratitude and awe the Eucharistic face of the Risen Christ who victoriously leads us past all obstacles of this earthly life to share in his life for a glorious eternity, a life of which the Eucharistic banquet is a pledge and foretaste. Every decade also includes a suggested intention of gratitude for the mystery of the Eucharist.

1. Jesus Rises from the Dead (Jn 20:1–10)

The Eucharistic Host that we receive and adore is the glorious Body, Blood, soul, and divinity of the Risen Christ: the very Christ before whose majesty angels tremble and whose wounds pulse with love for us, and who has promised us, "I am the living bread that came down from heaven. Whoever eats of this bread will live forever; and the bread that I will give for the life of the world is my flesh" (Jn. 6:51).

In thanksgiving: *for the gift of every Holy Communion, and the nourishment, strength, and life Jesus gives us in the Eucharist.*

2. Jesus Ascends into Heaven (Mk 16:19–20)

Before ascending into heaven, Jesus promises, "Behold, I am with you all days, even to the consummation of the world." Jesus fulfills this promise in many ways in the Church, but the most striking is his astonishing gift of himself in the Eucharist at every Mass and his continual presence in the tabernacle!

In thanksgiving: *for the gift of Jesus' Real Presence in the Eucharist and his constant availability in tabernacles throughout the world.*

3. The Holy Spirit Descends on the Apostles (Ac 2:1–4)

The Acts of the Apostles tells us that Mary accompanies the apostles in prayer in the Upper Room, helping them prepare to receive the power and gifts of the Holy Spirit. We ask Mary, woman of the Eucharist and spouse of the Spirit, to help us cultivate greater receptivity to the Holy Spirit, who will set our hearts aflame so that we can fulfill Jesus' command at the Last Supper: "Love one another as I have loved you" (Jn. 15:12).

In thanksgiving: *for the transforming gifts of the Holy Spirit poured out at every Mass and in every Communion, enabling us to live a truly Eucharistic life of love and service.*

4. Mary Is Assumed, Body and Soul, into Heaven (Lk 1:48–49)

By taking on our humanity, Jesus blesses our human bodies with a special promise of heavenly glory, and he promises even more to those who receive the Bread of Life: "This is the bread that came down from heaven, not like that which your ancestors ate, and they died. But the one who eats this bread will live forever" (Jn. 6:58). Jesus anticipates this promise for his Mother in her Assumption, and thus reassures us that we, too, will be raised up on the last day.

In thanksgiving: *for the promise of eternal life that the Eucharistic Jesus gives us.*

5. Mary Is Crowned Queen of Heaven and Earth (2 Tm 2:12)

The Eucharist Banquet, a preview of the heavenly banquet, is our "pledge of future glory" and a foretaste of the salvation Jesus won for us in his paschal mystery. We could also say that Jesus' Eucharistic love for us is also a pledge and foretaste of the embrace of divine love that is heaven.

In thanksgiving: *for the salvation Jesus won for us and makes sacramentally present at every Eucharist.*

Eucharistic Mysteries of the Rosary

These Eucharistic mysteries, intended to be prayed as we do the traditional mysteries of the Rosary, are offered here as a help to contemplate one of the greatest mysteries of our faith: the Holy Eucharist.

1. Jesus Multiplies the Loaves and Fishes (Mk 6:30–44)

The hour is late. Jesus has been teaching the enormous crowd of people all day, breaking open for them the bread of God's word. His disciples approach Jesus with a request that precipitates this miracle foreshadowing the Eucharist:

When it grew late, his disciples came to him and said, "This is a deserted place, and the hour is now very late; send them away so that they may go into the surrounding country and villages and buy something for themselves to eat." But he answered them, "You give them something to eat." They said to him,

"Are we to go and buy two hundred denarii worth of bread, and give it to them to eat?" And he said to them, "How many loaves have you? Go and see." When they had found out, they said, "Five, and two fish." Taking the five loaves and the two fish, he looked up to heaven, and blessed and broke the loaves, and gave them to his disciples to set before the people; and he divided the two fish among them all. And all ate and were filled; and they took up twelve baskets full of broken pieces and of the fish. Those who had eaten the loaves numbered five thousand men. (Mk 6: 35–38, 41–44)

2. Jesus Gives the Bread of Life Discourse (Jn 6:22–71)

Having been filled with the miraculous loaves, the people want more. But are they ready for the fullness of life that Jesus wants to give them? Are we?

"Very truly, I tell you, whoever believes has eternal life. I am the bread of life. Your ancestors ate the manna in the wilderness, and they died. This is the bread that comes down from heaven, so that one may eat of it and not die. I am the living bread that came down from heaven. Whoever eats of this bread will live forever; and the bread that I will give for the life of the world is my flesh."

The Jews then disputed among themselves, saying, "How can this man give us his flesh to eat?" So Jesus said to them, "Very truly, I tell you, unless you eat the flesh of the Son of Man and drink his blood, you have no life in you. Those who eat my flesh and drink my blood have eternal life, and I will raise them up on the last day; for my flesh is true food and my blood is true drink. Those who eat my flesh and drink my blood abide in me, and I in them." (Jn 6: 47–56)

3. Jesus Institutes the Holy Eucharist (Lk 22:17–38)

Jesus' passion is about to begin, that great act of redemption carried out for love of us, but Jesus longs to do even more: he desires to perpetuate his redeeming act of love through his sacramental presence among us.

When the hour came, he took his place at the table, and the apostles with him. He said to them, "I have eagerly desired to eat this Passover with you before I suffer; for I tell you, I will not eat it until it is fulfilled in the kingdom of God." Then he took a cup, and after giving thanks he said, "Take this and divide it among yourselves; for I tell you that from now on I will not drink of the fruit of the vine until the kingdom of God comes." Then he took a loaf of bread, and when he had given thanks, he broke it and gave it to them, saying, "This is my body, which is given for you. Do this in remembrance of me." And he did the same with the cup after supper, saying, "This cup that is poured out for you is the new covenant in my blood." (Lk 22:14–20)

4. Jesus Sacrifices His Life for Us on Calvary (Jn 19:16–30)

The "Hour" has come: Jesus gives himself up for us, offering his life on the altar of the Cross to save us. This sacrifice is the great memorial of his love.

So they took Jesus; and carrying the cross by himself, he went out to what is called The Place of the Skull, which in Hebrew is called Golgotha. There they crucified him. . . .

Standing near the cross of Jesus were his mother, and his mother's sister, Mary the wife of Clopas, and Mary Magdalene. When Jesus saw his mother and the disciple whom he loved standing beside her, he said to his mother, "Woman, here is your son." Then he said to the disciple, "Here is your mother." And from that hour the disciple took her into his own home.

After this, when Jesus knew that all was now

finished, he said (in order to fulfill the scripture), "I am thirsty." A jar full of sour wine was standing there. So they put a sponge full of the wine on a branch of hyssop and held it to his mouth. When Jesus had received the wine, he said, "It is finished." Then he bowed his head and gave up his spirit. (Jn 19:16–18, 25–30)

5. Jesus Appears to the Disciples on the Way to Emmaus (Lk 24:13–35)

It's the third day after the Crucifixion, but the truth of the Resurrection has not yet hit home for the disciples. Unrecognized, Jesus catches up with two discouraged disciples as they leave Jerusalem, revealing himself only at the end in the "breaking of bread."

Beginning with Moses and all the prophets, he [Jesus] interpreted to them the things about himself in all the scriptures. As they came near the village to which they were going, he walked ahead as if he were going on. But they urged him strongly, saying, "Stay with us, because it is almost evening and the day is now nearly over." So he went in to stay with them. When he was at the table with them, he took bread, blessed and broke it, and gave it to them. Then their eyes were opened, and they recognized him; and he vanished from their sight. They said to each other, "Were not our hearts burning within us while he was talking to us on the road, while he was opening the scriptures to us?" That same hour they got up and returned to Jerusalem; and they found the eleven and their companions gathered together. They were saying, "The Lord has risen indeed, and he has appeared to Simon!" Then they told what had happened on the road, and how he had been made known to them in the breaking of the bread. (Lk 24:27–35)

Litany of Loreto

Lord, have mercy on us.

R̹. *Christ, have mercy on us.*

Lord, have mercy on us. Christ, hear us.

R̹. *Christ, graciously hear us.*

God the Father of heaven, R̹. *have mercy on us.*

God the Son, Redeemer of the world, R̹.

God the Holy Spirit, R̹.

Holy Trinity, one God, R̹.

Holy Mary, R̹. *pray for us.*

Holy Mother of God, R̹.

Holy Virgin of virgins, R̹.

Mother of Christ, ℟.

Mother of the Church, ℟.

Mother of mercy, ℟.

Mother of divine grace, ℟.

Mother of hope, ℟.

Mother most pure, ℟.

Mother most chaste, ℟.

Mother inviolate, ℟.

Mother undefiled, ℟.

Mother most amiable, ℟.

Mother most admirable, ℟.

Mother of good counsel, ℟.

Mother of our Creator, ℟.

Mother of our Redeemer, ℟.

Virgin most prudent, ℟.

Virgin most venerable, ℟.

Virgin most renowned, ℟.

Virgin most powerful, ℟.

Virgin most merciful, ℟.

Virgin most faithful, ℟.

Mirror of justice, ℟.

Seat of wisdom, ℟.

Cause of our joy, ℟.

Spiritual vessel, ℟.

Vessel of honor, ℟.

Singular vessel of devotion, ℟.

Mystical rose, ℟.

Tower of David, ℟.

Tower of ivory, ℟.

House of gold, ℟.

Ark of the covenant, ℟.

Gate of heaven, ℟.

Morning star, ℟.

Health of the sick, ℟.

Refuge of sinners, ℟.

Solace of migrants, ℟.

Comforter of the afflicted, ℟.

Help of Christians, ℟.

Queen of angels, ℟.

Queen of patriarchs, ℟.

Queen of prophets, ℟.

Queen of apostles, ℟.

Queen of martyrs, ℟.

Queen of confessors, ℟.

Queen of virgins, ℟.

Queen of all saints, ℟.

Queen conceived without original sin, ℟.

Queen assumed into heaven, ℟.

Queen of the holy Rosary, ℟.

Queen of families, ℟.

Queen of peace, ℟.

Lamb of God, who takes away the sins
of the world, ℟. *spare us, O Lord.*

Lamb of God, who takes away the sins
of the world, ℟. *graciously spare us, O Lord.*

Lamb of God, who takes away the sins
of the world, ℟. *have mercy on us.*

℣. Pray for us, O holy Mother of God,

℟. That we may be made worthy of
the promises of Christ.

Let us pray.

Grant, we beseech you, O Lord God, that we your
servants may enjoy lasting health of mind and body,
and by the glorious intercession of the Blessed Mary,

ever Virgin, be delivered from present sorrow and enter into the joy of eternal happiness. Through Christ our Lord. Amen.

Our Lady of the Most Blessed Sacrament

Our Lady of the most Blessed Sacrament, Mother and Model of Adorers, pray for us who have recourse to you.

Saint Peter Julian Eymard

The Angelus

℣. The angel of the Lord declared unto Mary.
℟. And she conceived of the Holy Spirit.
Hail Mary . . .

℣. Behold the handmaid of the Lord.
℟. Be it done unto me according to thy word.
Hail Mary . . .

℣. And the Word was made flesh.
℟. And dwelt among us.
Hail Mary . . .

℣. Pray for us, O holy Mother of God.
℟. That we may be made worthy of the promises of Christ.

Let us pray.

Pour forth, we beseech thee, O Lord, thy grace into our hearts; that we, to whom the Incarnation of Christ, thy Son, was made known by the message of an angel, may by his passion and Cross be brought to the glory of his Resurrection. Through the same Christ, our Lord. Amen.

Glory be to the Father . . .

Memorare

Remember, O most gracious Virgin Mary,
that never was it known
that anyone who fled to your protection,
implored your help, or sought your
    intercession
was left unaided.
Inspired with this confidence, I fly to you,
O Virgin of virgins, my Mother.
To you I come, before you I stand, sinful
    and sorrowful.
O Mother of the Word Incarnate, despise not my
    petitions,
but in your mercy hear and answer me. Amen.

We Fly to Your Protection

We fly to your protection,
O holy Mother of God;
Despise not our petitions in our necessities,
but deliver us always from all dangers,
O glorious and blessed Virgin. Amen.

Oldest known prayer to the Virgin

Hail, Holy Queen

Hail, holy Queen, Mother of mercy, our life, our sweetness, and our hope! To you we cry, poor banished children of Eve; to you we send up our sighs, mourning and weeping in this valley of tears. Turn then, most gracious advocate, your eyes of mercy toward us, and after this our exile, show unto us the blessed fruit of your womb, Jesus. O clement, O loving, O sweet Virgin Mary.

O Mary, My Queen

O Mary, my Queen, I cast myself into the arms of your mercy.

I place my soul and body under your blessed care and your special protection.

I entrust to you all my hopes and consolations, all my anxieties and sufferings, my entire life, and the final hours of my life.

Through your most holy intercession, grant that all of my works may be directed and carried out according to your will and the will of your divine Son. Amen.

Saint Louis de Montfort

Act of Consecration

Receive me, O Mary, Mother, Teacher, and Queen, among those whom you love, nourish, sanctify, and guide, in the school of Jesus Christ, the Divine Master.

You see in the mind of God those whom he calls, and for them you have special prayers, grace, light, and consolations. My Master, Jesus Christ, entrusted himself wholly to you from the Incarnation to the Ascension. For me this is doctrine, example, and an ineffable gift. I too place myself entirely into your hands. Obtain for me the grace to know, imitate, and love ever more the Divine Master, Way, Truth, and Life. Present me to Jesus, for I am an unworthy sinner, and I have no other recommendation to be admitted to his school than your recommendation. Enlighten my mind, fortify my will, sanctify my heart during this year of my spiritual work, so that I may profit from this great mercy, and may say at the end: "I live now not I, but Christ lives in me."

Blessed James Alberione

Prayer to the Mother of All Adorers

O Mary, teach us the life of adoration!
Teach us to see, as you did, all the mysteries and
    all the graces in the Eucharist;
to live over again the Gospel story and to read it
in the light of the Eucharistic life of Jesus.
Remember, our Lady of the most Blessed
    Sacrament,
that you are the Mother of all adorers
    of the Holy Eucharist.

Saint Peter Julian Eymard

Hail Mary, of Whom Was Born Our Eucharistic Jesus

Hail Mary, of whom was born our Eucharistic Jesus!

Blessed are you among women, O Mary, and blessed is our Eucharistic Jesus, the fruit of your womb!

O Mary, fruitful vine that has given us the Eucharistic Wine, be forever blessed!

Hail Mary, vessel of purest gold, containing sweetness itself, our Eucharistic Jesus, the Manna of our souls!

O Mary, you are the true mystical table upon which we find the delicious food for our souls, Jesus in the Eucharist.

O Heart of Mary, magnificent throne of the hidden God, be exalted to the heights of the heavens!

O Mary, Mother of fair love, make us love Jesus in the Blessed Sacrament as you love him!

O Mary, give us Jesus Christ now and at the hour of our death.

Aspirations encouraged
by Saint Peter Julian Eymard

Prayer to Increase Eucharistic Devotion

O Virgin Mary, our Lady of the Blessed Sacrament, you who are the glory of the Christian people, joy of the universal Church, and salvation of the whole world, pray for us and awaken in all believers a lively devotion toward the most Holy Eucharist, that they may be made worthy to receive Communion daily.

With you may I adore, thank, supplicate, and console the most sacred and beloved Eucharistic Heart of Jesus!

Saint Peter Julian Eymard

Invocation for the Eucharistic Kingdom of Christ

℣. Pray for us, O Virgin Immaculate, our Lady of the most Blessed Sacrament,

℟. That the Eucharistic Kingdom of Jesus Christ may come through us!

Saint Peter Julian Eymard

O Mary, Make Me an Apostle

O Mary, Queen of Apostles, make me an apostle who bears God in my soul and radiates him to those around me. Fill my heart with such an intense love of God that I cannot keep it within myself but must communicate it to others. Make me a vessel capable of bearing Jesus Christ, that he may use me to shed light in the darkness.

O Mother, make me a temple of the Holy Trinity so that all my words, actions, prayers, gestures, and attitudes may speak of the God whom I so love. Make me an apostle, O Mary, like the great Apostle Paul. Amen.

Based on a prayer of Blessed James Alberione

Prayer of Entrustment

Mary, Queen of Apostles,
pray for us your children
who entrust ourselves entirely to you.
Pray for us so that we may never offend Jesus,
but may love him with all our hearts.
Beneath your mantle, O Mother,
we your children take refuge daily.
Make us all yours.

All that we have is yours.
You are our great teacher.
Teach us, guide us, sustain us,
defend us from every danger
as you have done until now.
And after this our exile
show us Jesus,
the blessed fruit of your womb.

Venerable Thecla Merlo, FSP

Prayer to Mary for Families

Come, Mary, and dwell in every family, which we consecrate to you.

May all families receive you with joy. May they welcome you with the same affection with which the apostle John brought you into his home after the death of your Son, Jesus.

Obtain for each family member the spiritual graces that they need, just as you brought grace to the home of Zechariah and Elizabeth.

Obtain material graces as well, just as you obtained the transformation of water into wine for the newlyweds at Cana.

Keep sin far away from every household. Be for each family light, joy, and sanctification, as you were in the family of Nazareth.

Obtain for family members an increase in faith, hope, and love, and a deeper spirit of prayer.

May Jesus, Way, Truth, and Life, dwell in every home!

Inspire everyone to follow their call and may they all be reunited in heaven one day.

Based on a prayer of Blessed James Alberione

Benediction

I put before you
the one great thing
to love on earth:
the Blessed Sacrament.
There you will find romance,
glory, honor, fidelity,
and the true way
of all your loves upon earth,
and more than that.

—*J. R. R. Tolkien*[13]

Because Christ himself is present in the Sacrament of the altar, he is to be honored with the worship of adoration (see the *Catechism of the Catholic Church*, no. 1378). Adoration can be brief or long or even extended throughout the day with adorers taking turns before the Blessed Sacrament.

Often adoration begins with exposition: The sacred Host is removed from the tabernacle by a priest, deacon, or designated minister and placed in a monstrance, then set upon the altar for all to see and worship. The minister incenses the Host, and a hymn honoring Jesus in the Eucharist is sung.

Benediction comes at the close of adoration: The celebrant again kneels before the altar and incenses the most Blessed Sacrament. The "Tantum Ergo" or another hymn of Eucharistic adoration is sung. The celebrant prays and the people respond. He then blesses the people with the sacred Host. The Divine Praises are recited together, and the Blessed Sacrament is returned to the tabernacle, while those present sing a hymn of Eucharistic praise.

O Saving Victim

O saving Victim, opening wide,
The gate of heaven to man below!
Our foes press on from every side;
Thine aid supply, thy strength bestow.

To Thy great name be endless praise,
Immortal Godhead, one in Three;
Oh, grant us endless length of days,
In our true native land with thee. Amen.

O Salutaris Hostia

O salutaris Hostia
Quae coeli pandis ostium!
Bella premunt hostilia,
Da robur, fer auxilium!

Uni trinoque Domino
Sit sempiterna gloria,
Qui vitam sine termino
Nobis donet in patria. Amen.

Saint Thomas Aquinas

Humbly Let Us Voice Our Homage

Humbly let us voice our homage
for so great a sacrament:
let all former rites surrender
to the Lord's new Testament;
what our senses fail to fathom
let us grasp through faith's consent!

Glory, honor, adoration
let us sing with one accord!
Praised be God, almighty Father;
praised be Christ, his Son, our Lord;

praised be God, the Holy Spirit;
Triune Godhead be adored! Amen.

The following verse and response may be added:

℣. You have given them bread from heaven
(alleluia).

℟. Having all sweetness within it (alleluia).

Let us pray.

O God, who in this wonderful Sacrament have left us a memorial of your Passion, grant us, we pray, so to revere the sacred mysteries of your Body and Blood that we may always experience in ourselves the fruits of your redemption. Who live and reign forever and ever. Amen.

Tantum Ergo

Tantum ergo sacraméntum
Venerémur cérnui:
Et antíquum documéntum
Novo cedat rítui:
Praestet fides suppleméntum
Sénsuum deféctui.

Genitóri, Genitóque
Laus et jubilátio,

Salus, honor, virtus quoque
Sit et benedíctio:
Procedénti ab utróque
Compar sit laudátio. Amen.

℣. Panem de cælo præstitísti eis (alleluia).
℟. Omne delectaméntum in se habéntem
(alleluia).

Orémus.

Deus, qui nobis sub sacraménto mirábili, passió-
nis tuæ memóriam reliquísti: tríbue, quæsumus, ita
nos córporis et sánguinis tui sacra mystéria venerári,
ut redemptiónis tuæ fructum in nobis iúgiter sentiá-
mus. Qui vivis et regnas cum Deo Patre in unitáte
Spíritus Sancti Deus, in sæcula sæculórum. Amen.

Saint Thomas Aquinas

After Benediction

The Divine Praises

Blessed be God.
Blessed be his holy name.
Blessed be Jesus Christ, true God and true man.

Blessed be the name of Jesus.

Blessed be his most Sacred Heart.

Blessed be his most precious Blood.

Blessed be Jesus in the most Holy Sacrament of the altar.

Blessed be the Holy Spirit, the Paraclete.

Blessed be the great Mother of God, Mary most holy.

Blessed be her holy and Immaculate Conception.

Blessed be her glorious Assumption.

Blessed be the name of Mary, Virgin and Mother.

Blessed be Saint Joseph, her most chaste spouse.

Blessed be God in his angels and in his saints.

Acknowledgments

Scripture where indicated is taken from the *New American Bible*, revised edition © 2010, 1991, 1986, 1970 Confraternity of Christian Doctrine, Washington, D.C., and are used by permission of the copyright owner. All rights reserved. No part of the New American Bible may be reproduced in any form without permission in writing from the copyright owner.

English translations of *Te Deum Laudamus*, © 1998, English Language Liturgical Consultation (ELLC), and used by permission. www.englishtexts.org.

"Novena of Grace" from the book *Hearts On Fire: Praying With the Jesuits* by Father Michael Harter, S.J. Used with permission: © The Institute of Jesuit Studies, Chestnut Hill, MA. All rights reserved.

Excerpts from *The Confessions of Saint Augustine* by St. Augustine, translated by John K. Ryan, copyright © 1960 by Penguin Random House LLC. Copyright renewed © 1988 by Winona Nation and Savings Bank. Used by permission of Doubleday, an imprint of the Knopf Doubleday Publishing Group, a division of Penguin Random House LLC. All rights reserved.

A profound thanks to all the Daughters of Saint Paul who contributed in a big way to this prayer book, whether the current or earlier editions. A very special thanks to Sister Mary Leonora Wilson, who helped with the compilation and contributed some beautiful prayers, and to Sister Mary Mark Wickenhiser, who provided many of the introductions.

Thanks also to the many sisters who provided original prayers or source material, including: Sister Mary Emmanuel, FSP, who translated the prayer, "O Immense Love" by Saint Alphonsus de Liguori; Sister D. Thomas Halpin, FSP; Sister Sharon Anne Legere, FSP; ; Sister Virginia Richards, FSP; Sister Patricia Shaules, FSP; Sister Mary Domenica Vitello, FSP; Sister Giovannamaria Carrara, FSP; Sister Gloria Bordeghini, FSP.

Unless otherwise noted, all prayers are from traditional sources.

Prayers by Blessed James Alberione are primarily from *The Prayers of the Pauline Family* (Daughters of Saint Paul, Boston. Approved for private use. All rights reserved.) Other prayers and writings are from out of print, privately published, or non-published translations. Writings of Blessed James Alberione that are currently available in English can be found at: https://operaomnia.alberione. org/en.

Notes

1. Blessed James Alberione, *Christ Lives in Me* (Boston: Pauline Books and Media, 2003), 50–51.

2. Saint Maria Faustina Kowalska, *Diary of Saint Maria Faustina Kowalska: Divine Mercy in My Soul* (Stockbridge, MA: Marian Press, 2005), no. 1692.

3. Saint Padre Pio, "Stay with Me, Lord," in *The Essential Handbook of Sacraments* (Liguori, MO: Liguori, 2001), 152.

4. John J. Cardinal Carberry, "Act of Adoration," in *Reflections and Prayers for Visits with Our Eucharistic Lord* (Boston: Pauline Books & Media, 2017), 8–9.

5. Victoria Schneider, comp. and trans., *The Bishop of the Abandoned Tabernacle: Saint Manuel González García* (New York: Scepter, 2018), 56.

6. Faustina, *Diary*, no. 1794.

7. Saint Augustine, *The Confessions of St. Augustine*, trans. John K. Ryan (New York: Image Books, 1960), bk. 10 ch. XXVII.

8. Saint Hildegard of Bingen, "Repentance and Reunion," in *Prayers of Hildegard of Bingen*, ed. Walburga Storch, O.S.B., trans. Sharon Therese Nemeth (Cincinnati, OH: Saint Anthony Messenger Press, 2003), 64–65.

9. Saint Oscar Romero, *The Violence of Love* (Farmington, PA: Plough Publishing House, 1988), 154.

10. Pope Saint John Paul II, "Letter of his Holiness John Paul II to All the Priests on the Occasion of Holy Thursday 1979," The Holy See, no. 7, https://www.vatican.va/content/john-paul-ii/en/letters/1979/documents/hf_jp-ii_let_19790409_sacerdoti-giovedi-santo.html. Adapted into prayer by Marie Paul Curley, FSP.

11. Pope Saint John Paul II, *Evangelium Vitae*, The Holy See, March 25, 1995, https://www.vatican.va/content/john-paul-ii/en/encyclicals/documents/hf_jp-ii_enc_25031995_evangelium-vitae.html.

12. Saint Peter Julian Eymard, *Month of Our Lady of the Blessed Sacrament* (New York: Sentinel Press, 1903), 21–22.

13. J. R. R. Tolkien, *The Letters of J. R. R. Tolkien*, ed. Humphrey Carpenter with the assistance of Christopher Tolkien (New York: Houghton Mifflin, 1981), 53.

List of Contributors

Saint Margaret Mary Alacoque
Heart of Love

Blessed James Alberione
Act of Consecration: "Receive me, O Mary . . ."
Chaplet to Jesus Master, Way, Truth, and Life
God's Dream for Me
Invocations to the Eucharistic Heart of Jesus
O Mary, Make Me an Apostle
Prayer for the Gifts of the Holy Spirit
Prayer of Adoration: "Jesus, today's adoration . . ."
Prayer to Mary for Families
To Jesus, Good Shepherd: "Jesus, you are the Good
Shepherd . . ."

Saint Alphonsus de Liguori
O Immense Love!

Saint Anselm
Prayer for the Needs of Others

O Sacrament Most Holy

Te Deum

To Jesus Crucified

We Fly to Your Protection

Unknown Author

For Faith in the Real Presence

Litany of Reparation to the Most Holy Sacrament

Litany of the Eucharist

Litany of the Most Blessed Sacrament

Prayer of Presence "Lord, I come before you here . . ."

You Have First Loved Me

Sister Mary Leonora Wilson, FSP

Act of Reparation to the Most Blessed Sacrament

Chaplet of Eucharistic Adoration

Eucharistic Mysteries of the Rosary

Loving Lord, I Believe

Stations of the Cross

To My Guardian Angel, Companion in Adoration

Pauline
BOOKS & MEDIA

A mission of the Daughters of St. Paul

As apostles of Jesus Christ,
evangelizing today's world:

We are CALLED to holiness
by God's living Word and Eucharist.

We COMMUNICATE the Gospel message
through our lives and through all
available forms of media.

We SERVE the Church
by responding to the hopes and needs
of all people with the Word of God,
in the spirit of St. Paul.

For more information visit us at:
www.pauline.org

Special Bulk Prices Available!*

Get multiple copies of *Essential Eucharistic Adoration Prayers*, *Essential Healing Prayers for Peace and Strength*, and *Essential Spiritual Warfare Prayers for Protection and Deliverance* for gifts, parish groups, RCIA candidates and catechumens, friends, and family.

20 + for $6 each
50 + for $5 each
100 + for $4 each

For U.S. bulk orders, online ordering available at https://paulinestore.com/spiritual-warfare-prayers or visit your local Pauline Books & Media book store.

For Canadian bulk orders, online ordering available at https://paulinestore.ca/spiritual-warfare-prayers or visit our Pauline Books & Media book store in Toronto.

*Prices subject to change. Bulk offer for trade and wholesale customers is net.